A Vegetable Gardener's Year

Also by Dirty Nails
HOW TO GROW YOUR OWN FOOD
A week-by-week guide to wild life friendly fruit and vegetable gardening

'This delightful book is a practical guide to enjoying the growing as much as the eating of your own food. It would be a stimulating book to encourage a beginner but being informative on many levels it is a really rewarding read for all who are willing to get their nails dirty.' *Reader review*

'What a wonderful book I have just read! It reads like a novel with the main character being 'Dirty Nails'. And what is it? A gardening book!! But it is more than that – wildlife, histories of various vegetables, soil information and for both the experienced and inexperienced gardener a week-by-week guide to planning, sowing, looking after and finally harvesting your very own veggies. Beautifully laid out and with a comprehensive contents page and extensive index, this is DEFINITELY one for the Gardener's library.' *Reader review*

'A delightful read. A "must" for ANY gardener. I felt so sad when I turned the page for the last week of January and found the year's week-by-week guide had finished. I wanted to just start all over again!' *Reader review*

'It is easy to imagine this book being consulted in garden sheds and allotment huts the length of the land, well thumbed in pursuit of another nugget of wisdom or vital piece of guidance from Dirty Nails. The sort of book any gardener would enjoy reading from cover to cover on a rainy afternoon.' *Fosse Way Magazine*

'A gardening book has got to be different, How to Grow Your Own Food is just that. This is a thoroughly enjoyable book which you could read at one sitting and delve into week by week.' *Mid Sussex Times*

'Packed with handy hints on wildlife-friendly fruit and veg gardening.' *Amateur Gardening*

'Thanks to his simple, down-to-earth style and chatty text, Dirty Nails is well worth a read. A delightful walk through the veg garden year, this book will be invaluable to anyone who's still finding their feet amid the excitement of growing their own food.' *Garden News*

'A 208-pager filled with fascinating facts and useful jobs for each week of the year.' *North Devon Journal*

'A book, that down-to-earth gardeners will love. Anyone will learn a lot from his honest-to-goodness book.' *Organic Gardening*

'For any wannabe fruit and veg grower.' *Kitchen Garden*

'Every so often a book comes along that blows all that out of the water. This book is an absolute 'must have' for anyone serious about growing their own produce. Refreshing, easy to read in one sitting or to dip in and out of as a reference work, this book really does tick all the boxes. Plain common sense, humour and an amazing eye for detail.' *Grow It!*

'The detailed week by week commentary make it seem like the author "Dirty Nails" is standing right beside you giving you interesting and practical tips and advice throughout the year. It is an excellent inspiring book for both beginners and experienced gardeners alike.' *www.organic-gardening-tips.co.uk*

'A refreshing alternative to many of the glossy publications offered by garden centres and the like. A very tasty read!' *Dorset Wildlife Trust Magazine*

'This book does exactly what it claims to do. It has two pages for each week in the year all packed with information. The writing style is amusing from beginning to end and so easy to read. Over a year this book would give the amateur gardener a huge amount of information in an amusing and easily readable form. We thoroughly recommend it for gardeners and also as a birthday or Christmas present.' *Gardenaction*

Spring Hill is an imprint of How To Books Ltd.
Send for a free copy of the latest catalogue to:

howtobooks

Spring Hill House, Spring Hill Road
Begbroke, Oxford OX5 1RX, United Kingdom
info@howtobooks.co.uk
www.howtobooks.co.uk

A Vegetable Gardener's Year

'Dirty Nails'
of *The Blackmore Vale Magazine*

SPRING HILL

Published by Spring Hill, an imprint of How To Books Ltd.
Spring Hill House, Spring Hill Road
Begbroke, Oxford OX5 1RX United Kingdom
Tel: (01865) 375794
Fax: (01865) 379162
info@howtobooks.co.uk
www.howtobooks.co.uk

British Library Cataloguing in Publication Data
A catalogue record of this book is available from the British Library

ISBN: 978 1 905862 22 1

Produced for How To Books by Deer Park Productions, Tavistock, Devon
Designed and typeset by Mousemat Design Ltd
Printed and bound by Bell & Bain Ltd., Glasgow

NOTE: The material contained in this book is set out in good faith for general guidance and no liability can be accepted for loss or expense incurred as a result of relying in particular circumstances on statements made in the book. Laws and regulations are complex and liable to change, and readers should check the current position with relevant authorities before making personal arrangements.

Contents

Acknowledgements

Help and encouragement in the writing and production of this book has come from many quarters. The author would especially like to thank the following:

Everyone at How To Books, without whom there would still only be dreams.

Mrs Nails, for her wonderfully supportive love, patience and shared thrill of gardening and food.

Mum and Dad, for being the best parents anyone could wish for, proof reading skills, unconditional love, and recipes from around the world.

Helen Hashman, for her beautifully simple recipes and feeding me so thoughtfully whenever I see her.

Elizabeth and Derek James, for years of unfailing friendship and generosity to animals and people.

Angela King of Common Ground, who told me to 'just keep writing'.

Colin Lea, for his delicious and easy Cashew Nut Curry recipe.

Douglas Childs, for his brilliant artwork.

Introduction

This book is for gardeners and nature-lovers everywhere. A 'grow your own' manual, recipe book and uniquely personal account of the changing year, it tells the tale of first-hand experience and observations from an author who has real affection for his subjects and locality.

Journeying week-by-week through the vegetable and fruit growing calendar, this mix of practical advice, humour and detailed study of natural history on the plot will satisfy armchair gardeners and full-on enthusiasts alike.

Thought provoking, inspiring, occasionally challenging, A Vegetable Gardener's Year is a book that can be taken to bed as an end of day muse or get dog-eared and dirty as an essential aid to cultivating and cooking home-grown food.

DOUGLAS CHILDS

Douglas Childs is a retired landscape architect living in Shaftesbury, Dorset. With its rich variety of buildings and unusual topography, this is an ideal habitat for one with a life-long interest in architecture and its relationship with the landscape. Like most designers, Douglas can never quite retire and needs little encouragement to go wild with a pen.

You will find his illustrations of local Dorset landmarks on pages xiv, 3, 14, 21, 55, 67, 70, 121, 128, 142, 146, 152, 155, 160, 169, 178 and 188.

A Vegetable
Gardener's Year

In the Garden

February 1st Week

Frogs & Bonfires

With the air full of springtime promise, this is an ideal time to have a bonfire. Dirty Nails has been burning up his woody waste and non-compostables in readiness for the exciting weeks ahead. He is always mindful of the fact that frogs like to rest up in twiggy piles. When he needs to have a burn up, Dirty Nails starts his fire a short distance from the rubbish. In this way he ensures that he is unlikely to incinerate any of his wide-mouthed friends, as the stuff for burning can be easily lifted with a garden fork and fed onto the blaze little by little. A certain amount of useful lengths of stick and other prunings are always kept back. These are tied into bundles and stored.

Cats

Freshly worked soil on the veg plot can be a magnet for cats. They like to scratch around and leave little 'presents' all over the place. Although Dirty Nails believes very much in a live-and-let-live approach to life, such feline antics can be a problem when seeds are being sown into open ground. To keep cats off seedbeds he places his sticks over the top at odd angles close together. This seems to do the trick, and does not impede the emerging seedlings.

On Disturbing a Queen Wasp

Whilst cleaning out his bird-boxes this week in order that the blue tits may have another brood or two in this coming season, Dirty Nails chanced upon a queen wasp hibernating inside one of them. She was hunched up in a foetal resting position, and remained un-moved as the gardener clumsily entered her hibernation chamber. Having hunted and scavenged their hectic way through last summer, queens such as this remain the sole survivors. They spend the winter months in quiet undisturbed places, their animation suspended. A nesting box is ideal. Apart from being beautiful, complex insects, wasps are useful in the garden. They account for masses of veg-devouring grubs and caterpillars. Dirty Nails was happy not to clean this particular box, and leave the queen in peace. However wasps do have an unfortunate knack of setting up home in the most inconvenient sites. With this in mind, and on Mrs Nails' request, he relocated the box and wasp from the side of a shed to high up in an out-of-the-way tree until that amazing call of nature urges her out to follow the instinctive ritual of millions of wasps before her.

FROM DIRTY NAILS' JOURNAL
MARKET DAY MORNING

I revived the flagging fire by dismantling, rebuilding, stoking, then turning the baffle plate shut for a long, slow burn. A cold snap may be in the offing, although these days the weather and temperatures fluctuate so much that there is no way of being entirely sure. I got fully coated-up prior to a trip to the wood pile, then ditched the heavy outer layer in my shed due to over-heating. And all this before 6.30 am at the beginning of February.

Up in town, market day emerges from the dark. The High Street will be active. I'll look for my mate from Stour Row, an old boy who tends a long, thin garden, with delphiniums on the road just before Jolliffes Farm. This is the chap who I acknowledged when arriving in this place fifteen years previous, with whom I always share a nod and wink. Ever since I began travelling back and fore past his cottage garden we have been on these terms. He would return my flashes, toots or waves by looking up, raising a hand and crooked finger, with a half-smile and glint in his eye. And do you know what? For a newcomer it was great to be on this level with a stranger.

Except he is no longer a stranger. His is one of the faces I look forward to seeing on a Thursday in town. He will be standing with his father and son mates on the flower stall, while the busy folk do their rounds. Clocking Geoff is one of the highlights of my day, and I am looking forward to it already.

Jobs to do this Week

In the Greenhouse

- Check over plants.

- Keep greenhouse well ventilated in mild weather.

- Have a sort and tidy in preparation for spring sowing (soon!).

On the Plot

- Clear and compost decaying lower leaves from Brussels sprouts (these can fruitfully be placed in the bottom of a bean trench).

- Import bundles of twiggy hazel faggots and store for various uses to come.

- Swill out and clean buckets, pots and such like which are loitering in corners or presenting trip hazards.

- Potter, tidy, mooch.

- Compost spent Brussels sprout plants (bash the woody stems into a pulp with a hammer).

- Hand weed elephant garlic.

- Clear a space against a sunny wall for strawberry production in barrels.

- Purchase and plant fruit trees (apples and pears, for example).

- Weed carefully around emerging rhubarb.

- Weed amongst purple sprouting broccoli.

- Clear and weed plot edges.

- Clean and maintain, or construct from scratch, paths.

In the Garden

February 2nd Week

Pond Action

The ponds are now a mass of heaving frogs, groaning and croaking as Dirty Nails passes them daily on his way up to the vegetable patch. Their numbers have been swelling over the last week or so and are reaching the point where the laying of their jelly-like blobs of spawn is imminent.

For Dirty Nails, who as a nature-friendly tender of the land holds frogs in the highest esteem, this time of year is most exciting. The fat females carry smaller males on their backs in a position known as 'amplexus'. The males hold on tightly with their front legs clasped around the necks of their spawn-laden partners, aided by rough pads of skin that develop below their thumbs and give them a tight grip.

Until that magic moment arrives, and it could be tonight, they rest in the thick weed. Pairs of heads poke out into the air as they bide their time, then duck down in unison as the heavy-footed gardener walks by.

Cabbages for Mid-Summer

While he waits for the frogs to lay their eggs, Dirty Nails has been planting summer cabbages. Sown now indoors in trays of moist compost, early varieties such as F1 Spitfire and Greyhound could be ready for eating as early as June.

He pops the pin-head sized brown or black seeds into trays to a depth of no more than ½ inch (1½ cm), covers, and firms gently. A little tipple of water is given. The would-be cabbages are placed on a windowsill or in the greenhouse to germinate.

When they have reached 3 or 4 inches (8-10 cm) in height, Dirty Nails will transplant the seedlings outside into firm, sunny soil. Here they should grow on speedily for cropping in mid-summer.

One reason why Dirty Nails favours these quick-growing brassicas is that they can be nurtured and harvested early in the season before white butterflies are causing too much cabbage damage.

FROM DIRTY NAILS' JOURNAL
OLD BROW

OLD BROW IS A BIG old-fashioned family house tucked away down a short gravel drive on a tight and narrow bend at the very corner of Bimport and St Johns Hill. Set in amazing grounds of considerable size, it looks out over the Blackmore Vale, beyond the wooded crowns of Duncliffe and stretching away past Gillingham. The house lies empty, curtains drawn and moss gathering on the edges outside. The *Yellow Pages*, still unwrapped, tossed down near the door.

It's the sort of dwelling that conjures images of large families, busyness and noise. It is condemned. Not unsound or dangerous but sitting on a plot worth a fortune. Therein lies the reason why both home and gardens have the feel of wildness, nether-lands on the change from lovingly tended homestead to rough brambly thicket. The property is up for development, a dense crowding of homes on this site to line a few pockets thickly. In the run up to the ball and chain I have visited this plot frequently to taste the last vestiges of how it was.

I'm sitting by the cobwebbed summerhouse on a garden chair taken from inside an unlocked shed. Grass is tussocky and unmown and white-flowered heather beds sprawl towards the pond. A rickety footbridge over this has become slippery

through lack of passage and two slats are loose, but from it I can see newts in the shallows, tails wafting from the shadows. No frogs or spawn in this pool of water yet. It is still early in the year with plenty of time and opportunity to come.

In the gardens of Old Brow trees grow everywhere. Whoever designed the garden mixed a lot of conifers and deciduous. The effect is glorious. Spruce, pine, cypress of all shapes and sizes studded amongst beech and silver birch, eucalyptus and some amazing cherries. Cotoneaster and pussy willow turned into trees, shrubs breaking the boundaries of their borders, blackberries cascading over and through a barberry hedge smattered with clusters of deep yellow flowers. The wind from the southwest is noisily billowing in but the trees of Old Brow break it and filter it. A handsome group of Norway Spruce bend their 60 foot trunks and wave their dangling branches. The urgent tsip-tsip of titmice and alarm call of a blackbird are drowned almost out of earshot by the gusting gale. In a sheltered spot by the summerhouse I am resting, bathed in sunlight. The clouds move fast overhead as an ever-changing blanket of cover but the air down below is still, calmed by the plants, and suggests the feeling of being in some kind of secret garden time warp. The naturally occurring

OLD BROW
continued

successional transition of this abandoned plot from carefully tended few acres to woodland is tangible, but will come to nothing this time around. The magic of the place is doomed to change. Just like the newts in the pond and the frogs yet to arrive, other wildlife living in these grounds is either going to be destroyed or made homeless. Although any garden is entirely artificial, as nature takes back a neglected acre or two lines become increasingly blurred.

The wood pigeon that just alighted on the spreading bare branches of a cherry tree a few feet above my head was clearly not expecting a human visitor. I glanced up and our eyes met when the pigeon folded his wings and, almost settling, looked around. The bird was shocked enough to open them again and take off in virtually the same movement. The unexpected surprise is nothing to what is in the offing when heavy machinery and bulldozers move in. I wonder where the small birds will go then. And what of the pretty primroses, randomly bringing delicate patches of lemon-yellow to complement the vast array of greens? As a reflective passenger through this place I make a conscious effort to visually drink in the heady cocktail of beautiful, contrived but natural, forms.

Changes planned for rambling properties such as this one cause wildlife-friendly gardeners like me to worry about the creatures in the pond: where they will live, how they will manage amongst the diggers and their caterpillar tracks. This little delicately balanced body of water could be destroyed as easily as cracking an egg on the side of a bowl, its contents spilling out onto the earth with nowhere safe to go. And the badgers, whose elaborate complex of tunnels and runs radiate underneath and out, down, up and over a steep bank adjacent, will be affected. Although they are big enough to make someone stop and think, with the added bonus of legal protection, provisions for them are often overlooked as the land, their land, is parcelled up and portioned off. They are the original tenants but the wrong species to make a claim.

Of all the trees in Old Brow grounds, a cherry that stands between the house and badger slope is my favourite. The trunk equals four outstretched hand-spans across with a spreading root bole of double that. At three or four feet the crown begins, with three enormous mossy, lichen-encrusted branches spreading out at equal distances from each other. In places, these twist and split out in more smaller limbs, at times crossing back over themselves and fused together from years of continual touching.

The latticed scaffold of jumbled sticks and twigs, snaking outwards and in amongst as a clearly defined framework, is nowhere more than twelve feet high, but the crown spreads eleven paces across both ways. I must be forever stooping my head to avoid knocking it on the lowest limbs, thick as a man's leg. Outrageously stunning to look at, the shape of this tree is beautifully domed like a giant flat mushroom. Towards mid-February, abundant clusters of fat buds are starting to swell with reddy-brown scales showing pale green at their tips.

There is no start or finish to the natural order of things, just temporary closures and fresh beginnings. Individuals come and go, be they people, trees, foxes or crocuses, but the wheel keeps on turning as each day brings something different.

Jobs to do this Week

In the Greenhouse

- Sow French Breakfast radish, F1 Market Express turnip, Lobjoits Green Cos lettuce, F1 Spitfire and Greyhound cabbage.

- Place winter purslane and corn salad (in pots) outside during the day to harden off.

- Pot on black knapweed (grown from seed for insects, especially bees).

- Put all over-wintered strawberry plants outside unless the weather is really cold.

- In freezing weather take frost precautions with chitting potatoes by covering at night with horticultural fleece or newspaper.

On the Plot

- Continue to construct paths wherever these may be needed later in the season.

- Tidy up around the pond removing perennial weeds, but be mindful to leave enough cover to protect frogs on the move from cats.

- Potter gently.

- Last chance to clean out bird nesting boxes.

- Clear, weed and define plot edges.

- Hoe through Winter onions if conditions allow.

- Compost bashed-up Brussels sprout plants which have been fully harvested (including the delicious tops).

- Compost spent Swiss chard.

- Trim hedges around the plot.

- Take care when digging Jerusalem artichokes to meticulously remove every last tiny piece of tuber. Any bit left in the ground will grow again, which may interfere with subsequent crops.

- Lift remaining celeriac and leeks. 'Heel in' close to the kitchen.

- Plant a Victoria plum tree.

- Dig over ground where celeriac has been harvested.

- Clear weeds and grasses from around soft fruit bushes. Take care not to disturb any more than just below the soil surface as blackcurrants and gooseberries especially are shallow-rooted.

- Prune newly planted apple and pears by nipping off the tips of branches.

- Tidy and sort the shed!

In the Garden February 3rd Week

Sowing Strawberries

Dirty Nails has been in the greenhouse this week sowing strawberry seeds. He favours two varieties, Alpine and Temptation F1. The former is useful for planting outside in shady areas where it produces masses of small, intensely-flavoured fruits. Temptation F1 grows large, juicy, very sweet strawberries when cultivated in a sunny place. It will fruit this summer from a sowing now, and will crop especially heavily in the second and third years.

The seeds of these glorious-tasting beauties are tiny. Dirty Nails has to use tweezers to handle them. They are sown very thinly in trays of moist compost, barely ¼ inch (½ cm) deep. Patience is needed when growing strawbs from seed, as they can be slow germinators and developers. He keeps them in a sunny place, moist but not wet, in an unheated greenhouse, and does not expect his seedlings to be large enough to pot on for a couple of months. He won't plant them outside until mid-April or early May.

Tending Broads

Most of the broad beans that Dirty Nails planted outside in mid-October are showing 5 or 6 inches (15 cm) of healthy growth. The odd one has not germinated and a few are exhibiting signs of 'foot and root rot'. This shows as withered and blackened or dark brown lower leaves and stems. It is fatal to the affected broads but thankfully won't ruin the whole crop if spotted early. Dirty Nails finds that a few over-wintering broads always catch it but that losses are usually minimal. Any individual looking unhealthy is pulled up and burned.

Where there are spaces in his rows of broad beans, he plants fresh seeds to make up the gaps. Pushed in to a depth of 3 inches (7 cm), at 6 inch (15 cm) intervals, they will soon be growing strongly and prove useful in extending the cropping season.

FROM DIRTY NAILS' JOURNAL
INSECTS ON THE WING

The middle of February can feel more like April some mornings, as the shroud of mist is burned off by a bright sun set high in a sky of pure blue. Shadows lengthen. A wood pigeon calls lazily from within the leafless lime tree which stands enormous at the bottom of the plot. It is not yet noon, but on days like this so early in the year we may be blessed with such solar finery that bees are on the wing, bumbling about in search of early dandelions that wink shyly from the unmown edges. Soil is warming up already down on the allotment.

Standing up straight to take a rest from digging, I need to tilt my cap at an angle to shield the sun from my eyes.

A hoverfly buzzes past, then drops down onto the drooping splayed white flower of a snowdrop. Its shining fat abdomen pulsates as it takes sustenance, then works the flower next to it, climbs out on top, turns a circle and lifts off. There are lots of flying insects checking out everything. Alas, the flowers available are few and far between. But they are about. For the zigzagging seekers, this year's quest has begun.

Jobs to do this Week

In the Greenhouse

- Water seedlings and crops in pots.

- Cover early tomato seedlings with newspaper at night if the conditions outside are freezing.

- Take frost precautions with chitting spuds at night.

- Continue to keep the place clean and tidy.

On the Plot

- Keep clearing vegetation from around gooseberry bushes.

- Prune gooseberries by cutting out half the old stems.

- Dig over parsnip bed except areas where roots remain in the ground.

- Hoe down *Phacelia* grown as a green manure amongst autumn-sown broad beans to give the beans more light and see where seed has failed and needs re-sowing. Plant up these gaps.

- Compost the last Brussels sprout plants (smash stems with a hammer beforehand) and turn over the bed where they were.

- Define, clear and weed plot edges. Tease out as much couch as you are able and burn it.

- Stroll around your little piece of heaven and have a good think, planning for the season to come in your head or (better still) on paper.

- Collect old metal drums from the scrap yard. Use a grinder to cut slots, one horizontal with a vertical cut either end, to knock in and create lots of planting pockets around the circumference for growing strawberries. Pretty up with paint which is weatherproof and rustproof.

- Fill strawberry barrels with rich soil and/or compost

- Drape bubble wrap over Brown Turkey fig to protect from late winter frosts.

In the Garden February 4th Week

Boosting Winter Purslane

The winter purslane which Dirty Nails sowed towards the end of September has been producing masses of succulent leaves. He grew on some of the seedlings outside under jam-jars. These are beginning to fill up their make-shift cloches but are still on the rather small side. However, a dozen were transplanted into pots and have been kept in the greenhouse. These plants have been growing with great gusto, their pickings complementing many a meal and sandwich for the last two or three months. But they are to becoming a bit tired so Dirty Nails has been giving them a boost this week.

Dirty Nails has trimmed off the entire

rosette of fleshy leaves and removed the plants from their pots. In all cases the roots were wound round the inside, clogging the bottom of the 6 inch (15 cm) pots. He has teased out some of the root-ball and popped each purslane plant into a plastic trough filled with refreshed soil. Given 4 inch (10 cm) spacings, they have been nestled snugly into their new growing medium.

Having placed these close shaven tufts of tight growth in the sunniest spot in the garden, Dirty Nails is expecting them to throw out abundant fresh new leaves soon.

In Praise of Sycamores

Although the sycamore is dismissed by many as a weed tree, in fact it has many virtues and benefits to the environment. Grown as a specimen in a parkland or open setting, it reaches the highest echelons of tree beauty in respect of its shape and stature. Sycamore trees are vigorous growers all over Britain, robust and hardy. They can tolerate levels of air pollution in urban areas that would prove fatal to most other trees and are unaffected by salt-laden sea winds, which makes them ideal planting choices for exposed and coastal areas.

In open country their dense canopies are much sought after by livestock as shade from the summer sun, or shelter from rain. Wherever they are allowed to grow unhindered with space to develop, sycamores provide a wealth of associated insect life which in turn supports numerous bird species. Their seasonal early summer bounty of aphids is crucial for returning migrants who visit our shores to raise their young. After incredible journeys from all over the world, birds like swifts, house martins, and swallows, amongst others, depend on a glut of insects to replenish their energies.

Also known as the Great Plane, conventional wisdom states that sycamores were introduced to Britain from Continental Europe at least 400 years ago. However, this opinion is being questioned now. Differences in the fossilised pollen of field maples and sycamores are indistinguishable. Countries such as Denmark, for whom the sycamore was always thought of as an alien, have re-classified it as a native. Argument goes on in this country too, especially in the North, as to the true status of this tree.

The wood is easily worked and creamy-white with a fine grain that does not warp. It is ideal for furniture making, and traditionally used in the construction of stringed instruments. Formerly, sycamore wood was widely utilised in kitchen and domestic settings as spoons and utensils, butter pats and worktops.

The leaves are large and glossy, unfolding to a bright green which dulls as summer passes to autumn. When shed, they are easily gathered by hand or machine. Except where collected by the polluted sides of busy main roads, they will provide a rich and crumbly leaf mould in twelve months or so which is perfect for enriching allotment soils, gardens and municipal beds.

Their seeds are the spinning 'helicopters' which have fascinated generations of school children and are easy to grow. Potted into any decent soil, they will rapidly shoot up and produce their first set of leaves. The structure of this tree lends itself perfectly to the age-old custom of tree-climbing. In this respect, once beyond the vulnerable sapling stage sycamores become extremely popular with kids of all ages as one of nature's finest climbing frames and for making dens and tree houses.

Leafless in wintertime, sycamores are far from lifeless. The flaking, fissured bark of old trees provides cosy nooks and crannies for spiders and invertebrates. Mixed flocks of insect-eating birds, tits, nuthatches, tree creepers and more seek out these tasty morsels. They will work amongst the handsome network of branches to eke out a meagre ration. Where clean air prevails sycamores can become encrusted with tufts of lichen.

Hardy, vigorous, adaptable, tough, versatile. If sensitively and thoughtfully planted a sycamore can be a wonderful asset for a community. They may attain heights of 115 feet (35 metres) and live for 250 years, adding a fascinating arboreal dimension to any chosen environment. They cannot match the English oak when it comes to supporting wildlife, and the tulip tree offers far more in terms of colour variations as the seasons pass. But sycamores have their own outstanding qualities, some of which are described here. Dirty Nails wishes that this much maligned tree had a far more respected place amongst our towns, cities, coasts and countryside.

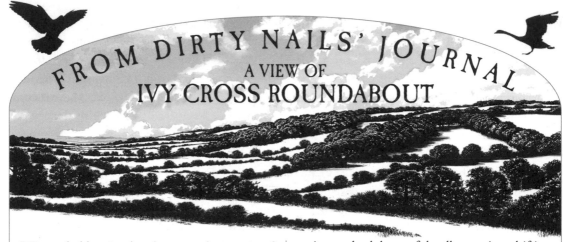

FROM DIRTY NAILS' JOURNAL
A VIEW OF
IVY CROSS ROUNDABOUT

Enough blue in the sky to make a pair of sailor's trousers. A bright warmth of sunshine that makes the laurel hedges shine and shadows stretch out across the verge into the path of coming, going, filtering-off and merging-in vehicles, pouring four ways with barely a gap enough to hear anything but machinery. Ivy Cross roundabout at the top of town. Busy, modern, cosmopolitan. Working men with carrier bags full of sandwiches, Coke and crisps. Refuelling and cranking up petrol-breathing dragons. Women, men in suits, checking the details at the pump. Hurrying over the forecourt to pay the price.

During a lull, plaintive mewing overhead. Five buzzards soaring, spiralling across the ether against a backdrop of hardly moving drifting banks of loose, fluffy, off-white clouds and changing shades of blue which darken slightly as the eye meanders higher. Then out of view as the straight-edged petrol station canopy blots them out. Jackdaws in groups of three or four, maybe twenty or more a few minutes before, and blackbirds playing chicken with the traffic between gardens either side of the main road. They rush and swoop across like missiles barely off the ground, then open their wings to slow and alight at an angle in the laurel and privet hedges. A big, but not enormous, beech tree grows in the midst of one, its smooth grey bark catching the sunlight on this mild day which holds the promise of spring.

Jobs to do this Week

In the Greenhouse

- Frost precautions at night for chitting spuds and tomato seedlings.

- Sow Greyhound cabbage, Anouk lettuce.

- Pot on Lobjoits Green Cos lettuce sown just after mid-January.

- Re-pot winter purslane into larger containers for greenhouse cultivation. Those to go outside can be planted into their final positions now.

On the Plot

- Dig over where cabbages grew.

- Where thatching straw was used to mulch an area for squashes last summer, turn this in.

- Apply a mulch of dry bracken to bases of broad beans if weather is hard.

- Check over the veg patch. Garlic and one or two shallots should be showing green sprouts.

- Compost Red Drumhead cabbages which are not firming up.

- Keep carefully digging Jerusalem artichokes.

February Veg on the Menu

Leaves and greens
Brussels sprout tops
Brussels sprouts (last)
Cabbage, January King
Cabbage, Pixie
Kale, Dwarf Green Curled
Kale, Thousandhead
Leaf beet
Swiss chard
Red cabbage
White sprouting broccoli

Roots, tubers & stems
Carrot
Celeriac
Jerusalem artichoke
Parsnip
Salsify, Sandwich Island
Scorzonera
Spuds, Pink Fir Apple (store)
Swede, Marian

Salads
Winter purslane
Corn salad
Lettuce, Lobjoits Green Cos

Onion tribe
Garlic (store)
Leek, Giant Winter
Onion (store)
Shallots (store)
Spring onion

Vegetable fruits
Squash (store, last one!)

In the Garden

March 1st Week

Preparing the Potatoes

When it comes to planting potatoes, Dirty Nails likes to have the ground well prepared beforehand. This means getting the planting site ready now. He plants his spuds in trenches with well-rotted manure, grass clippings, compost or leaf mould mixed into the bottom.

To this end, he has been marking out the rows with canes and string, then digging the trenches to the depth of one spit (the length of a spade head). He piles the soil carefully to one side. When working on sloping ground he always puts excavations to the top side. This will make 'earthing up' throughout the summer less of a strain. Organic matter to nourish the hungry growing spuds is then forked in to the bottom of the trenches. Early potato varieties appreciate 2 feet (60 cm) between rows. Maincrops need a bit more at 2½ feet (75 cm). Dirty Nails plants the chitted (pre-sprouted) tubers of Earlies a foot (30 cm) apart, and Maincrops at 1½ feet (45 cm) intervals.

With spuds being such an important crop, another advantage of preparation well before planting is that he can work out exactly how much of the veg patch will be devoted to them in the coming months. It's quite a big job, but easily accomplished when tackled methodically, a little bit at a time. With March being the unpredictable month that it is, Dirty Nails could be bending his back whilst sweating in a t-shirt, or wrapped up in a coat and scarf as sleet and snow falls around him. Whatever the weather, this job has a drastic visual effect on the garden. The ridge-and-furrow earth workings are a physical sign of the labour of love in progress.

Preparing for Kale

Now is a good time to sow kale indoors. Also known as 'borecole', this brassica is a traditional and reliable cropper which provides rich pickings of deeply crinkled leaves throughout the winter months. Treated like a cabbage in the kitchen, it tastes slightly more earthy than its cousin (not quite as sweet). Kale is extremely tough and hardy, well able to recover from cabbage white caterpillar predations in the summer and the harshest winter weather.

Dirty Nails sows his seeds singly to a depth of ½ inch (1½ cm) into 3 inch (7 cm) pots of moist compost. He gently firms in the small round brown seeds. Young kale plants will be planted outside around the middle of summer, ideally with 1½ feet (45 cm) spacings. Dirty Nails is a big fan of kale, sowing Pentland Brig and Westland Winter varieties now, then Dwarf Green Curled and Thousandhead (a prolific, smooth-leaved type) in April.

FROM DIRTY NAILS' JOURNAL
A BAD NIGHT FOR FROGS

Warm and damp weather, with thick mist shrouding town and lolling about in drifts out in the country, combine to make it a bad night tonight for frogs and toads. Mildness and moisture bring them out. The slick wetness of tarmaced runways proves an irresistible lure as they answer the instinctive call of their ancestral ponds and ditches. These are ancient creatures for whom evolution has not equipped a knowledge or fear of such unnatural environs. And so they sit there, gulping and blinking on an endless black lily-pad waiting, as only frogs do, for something to happen. And of course, something is always happening on the roads. The pause is only fleeting, a calm to be smashed by the four-wheeled storm that is crashing along even now with blinding illumination and a choking backwash.

Main roads and local neighbourhoods alike are littered with tiny shattered bodies squashed flat or laid out on their backs with little legs grasping thin air. Many more sit and wait their turn as wildlife-friendly drivers swerve or slowly pass right over the top, willing the travelling princes to get out of the line o' fire.

This evening a toad walks slowly in front, belly held high by warty legs as he strides both gingerly and determinedly at the same time. And why not? He, or she, is not designed to deal with these human atrocities. That the scale of massacre is not sustainable year on year, night after night, seems plainly obvious with a little simple arithmetic. How long have these amphibians been evolving to fit in perfectly with their world? Compare that with the speed of motorised technological advancement. They just do not mix well with traffic. Back-along in another time, at certain times of the year, byways in villages like Steeple Aston were thick with heaving soft amphibious bodies. In those days, when a horse and cart clopped frogs with every step, the scales were weighted very differently.

Jobs to do this Week

In the Greenhouse

- Take frost precautions with chitting spuds and seedlings if very cold at night.

- Check over daily.

- In trays sow Carentan 3 leek, Prinz and Giant Prague celeriac, Sugar Snap pea, tomato (Early Pak 7, Britain's Breakfast, Tumbler, Gardener's Delight), pepper (Yolo Wonder, Long Red Marconi, Ring o' Fire), Early Wonder beetroot, Great Lakes lettuce.

- In pots sow Westland Winter and Pentland Brigg kale, Wellington F1 and Evesham Special Brussels sprout, Marner Grufewi cabbage, French Breakfast radishes.

On the Plot

- Enlarge the plot by straightening out curved edges (straight edges are most practical for veg production).

- Calculate the space required for spuds and mark out rows with canes and string.

- Purchase more seed potatoes if you don't think you have enough.

- Start to dig trenches for spuds.

- Keep clearing and preparing weedy ground.

- Plant 6 inch (15 cm) lengths of horseradish root into deep pots.

In the Garden

Carrots

After half-a-dozen or so mild days on the trot, the soil is tangibly warmer. This pleases Dirty Nails, who has been patiently biding his time as far as outside planting is concerned. This week he has been sowing carrots. There are carrots for all seasons and soil types. For an early harvest on rich, loamy soil he plumps for a variety such as Jeanette F1. This Nantes hybrid produces lovely cylindrical roots, ripe for pulling from July onwards. Well before that, however, the thinnings will serve up the sweetest of treats either munched raw, Bugs Bunny style, or lightly steamed. On poor shallow soils he would be tempted to try his luck with a stump-rooted variety.

Carrots are fun to grow. They like a well worked bed, preferably manured the previous year. Dirty Nails forks in leaf mould to lighten it up, rakes to a fine tilth, and marks out his rows with canes and string a foot (30 cm) apart. A drill is made with his finger directly under the string to a depth of ½ an inch (1½ cm). The seeds sown into this. Carrot seeds are pin-head sized ovals with ridges running length-ways. For ease and accuracy of handling, Dirty Nails empties some of the seed packet contents into the palm of one hand and takes a small pinch from this with thumb and forefinger of the other. Each pinch is sprinkled thinly into the drill. It is easy to drop in clumps of seed by mistake if done in a hurry, so he takes his time to do a proper job.

Even-sowing of seed now makes for easier and less wasteful thinning out later. Thinning is an essential ongoing job with carrot cultivation, but for now Dirty Nails is content to cover over the drills gently with the back of his hand and water well with a rose on his can.

Developing carrots are prone to attack from the dreaded carrot fly, whose grubs will bore into and damage the roots. Whenever earth around the necks of growing carrots is disturbed these insects will sniff them out and lay their eggs in the area. Dirty Nails solves this problem by growing spring onions adjacent. The strong aroma from onions keeps the flies away and these crops grow well together as companions.

Spring Onions

Spring onions are not space-hungry, so Dirty Nails sows Ishikura and White Lisbon varieties in between his rows of carrots. Again, a shallow drill and even sowing is the order of the day. He uses a slow and steady hand to deposit the shiny black seeds. Spring onions do not require later thinning so the aim is to get them in evenly, not too thinly and not too thickly.

FROM DIRTY NAILS' JOURNAL
WINCOMBE LANE
LOOKING EAST

I am sitting beneath a hedge bank at the edge of Wincombe Lane Rec looking out towards Zig Zag and Breeze Hills. The sky is blue. White fluffy clouds move as slowly as the hands of a clock from right to left. A patchwork of fields lies before, studded with huge creamy-grey ash trees, hedges thick with briar, thorn, greenfinch, robin and more, looking 'mid-March gorgeous'. Tussocky grass, as befits pasture set aside for future building of homes and gardens, driveways and service roads, but currently adopted by half the town's dog walkers, is a jungle of pale green and yellow tufts stretching away like a wind-whipped sea.

An island of four limes stands proud in the middle, lending to the pastoral scene a thicket of sucker growth beneath their majestic, mature forms. More hedges and oak trees in the middle distance, with white plastic bags snared amongst the thorny windbreaks every now and then.

Mother Nature pays no heed to the condemned status of this piece of Southern England. As she threatens to roll out her lush and vibrant carpet of spring in front of us all, despite the chill wind, the darkness of the winter hedge lines is lightened a shade by billions of buds at the cusp of bursting. This is the reality of here and now, squatting in a hedge hollow surrounded by wild garlic, great tits, crisp packets and beer cans.

Jobs to do this Week

In the Greenhouse

- Frost precautions at night.

- Sow leaf beet and Swiss chard.

- Keep seedlings moist but not wet.

On the Plot

- Employ the hoe if weather conditions permit.

- Plan where to sow carrots and spring onions, and prepare this area.

- Prepare sunny ground for receiving Feltham First Early peas that were sown in protected pots during early December.

- Finish digging spud trenches.

- Apply wood ash to bed for main crop onions, rake in and tread the ground firm by doing the 'gardener's shuffle'.

- Harvest and use remaining leeks. Heel in the last of the crop near to the house.

- Plant out pot-grown Feltham First Early peas in prepared ground.

- Commence enriching spud trenches with well rotted leaf mould, compost, manure, or whatever good stuff is to hand (avoid cooked kitchen waste which may attract rodents).

- Sow Jeanette carrots and Ishikura spring

- Make seedling area cat-proof to stop felines from curling up on seed trays for a snooze or having a scratch and dig when 'helping' with chores!

onions.

- Gratefully receive unwanted clumps of perennial flowers such as Golden Rod from friends. Divide the root balls and plant in uncultivated corners and sunny places beside hedges for the benefit of wildlife and a colourful floral display later in the year.

- Plant double rows of Witkiem broad bean.

- On ground enriched for a previous crop (such as cabbages or potatoes) prepare a bed for root veg by digging and raking to a fine tilth.

- Remove plastic bottle cloches from corn salad and winter purslane.

- Keep carefully harvesting Jerusalem artichokes.

- Sow French Breakfast radishes.

- Give a very diluted liquid-feed to peas planted out earlier in the week, corn salad, winter purslane and standing crops of Dwarf Green Curled kale.

- Apply water generously to fruit trees.

In the Garden · March 3rd Week

First Early Potatoes

The potato planting season has arrived in Dirty Nails' veg patch. Although traditionally Good Friday was the day when workers countrywide got their spuds into the ground, he staggers his planting dates to accommodate different types of potato. It commences this week with Concorde, a First Early variety which should yield a heavy crop of oval spuds, creamy and moist inside with a smooth yellowy skin - a beautiful potato!

With the ground already prepared, it is simply a matter of placing the individual chitted tubers on the bottom of his leaf mould lined trenches at 1 foot (30 cm) intervals. He puts them all out along the rows, which are 2 feet (60 cm) apart, so he can see clearly where he is going to be planting. 6 inches (15 cm) is a good depth. Dirty Nails then employs a broken spade handle with a rounded end to make a hole to the desired depth, and carefully nestles a seed spud at the bottom of each one with the stout dark chits facing upwards.

The holes are filled in and a little extra soil is pulled into the trench with a swan-necked (or 'draw') hoe. Potatoes are both hungry and thirsty. Goodness previously worked into the planting trenches will feed them. Because there are often extended dry spells in spring these days, Dirty Nails gives them a jolly good watering too. Trenches are good for this. Not only do they accommodate a lot of compostables deep down, but they also ensure that liquid will be concentrated where it is most needed as his potatoes become established.

Peppers and Tomatoes

Peppers can be planted now in the greenhouse with a little heat, or on a kitchen window-sill. Dirty Nails cultivates Ring o' Fire, which is as hot as the name suggests, and Long Red Marconi, a juicy sweet-tasting pepper. He pops the flat round seeds into pots of moist compost to about ½ inch (1½ cm) depth. Peppers need warmth to germinate, so he covers the pots with glass or bubble-wrap to increase heat and humidity. Patience is needed because it can take some weeks for seeds to split open and that first pair of leaves to loop up and out of the soil.

Tomatoes like similar treatment. Although widely available for potting on at markets, Dirty Nails always grows his own from seed. There are loads of varieties. Two of his favourites are Gardener's Delight and Britain's Breakfast. The former produces long trusses of sweet cherry tomatoes. The latter grows larger, juicy fruits which are fabulous sliced and fried for the first meal of the day. Kept warm, seedlings will emerge within a fortnight.

Peppers and tomatoes crop well in a greenhouse and Dirty Nails will pot his seedlings up in due course into grow bags.

FROM DIRTY NAILS' JOURNAL

IN THE ROOKERY

The temperature has lifted and wind dropped. In the micro-climate of this scrap of woodland, approaching the latter days of March it may even be described as faintly mild. My back is to the prison, facing the wooded peaks of a creamy Duncliffe and that Saxon hilltop town away to the right. A twin-bladed helicopter sweeps in front and behind out of sight, barely off the ground and thunderously overbearing all else as it steers a course, resembling a giant deformed mechanical insect. Even now, minutes later, the chunter of those heavy rotary blades echo from away over yonder like the continual rhythmic rumble of distant thunder.

Then soothing cries of communally nesting rooks fill the air again. They sit atop the spindly branches of smooth-barked ash and sturdy-armed oaks, clinging to the twigs, rocking back and forth and bouncing in a gentle breeze high amongst a mass of football-sized nests, secured and artfully woven into goblet forks and junctions. As I pass beneath the colony of handsome, pale-faced black crows, they rise up in a loose and disintegrating crowd, noisily cawing and squawking at my alien presence. The birds soon rest again minutes later, confidently roosting and chatting amongst themselves. I park myself underneath, on a bare thorny bank spangled with the pebble-dash of their olive-and-white spoil. The bank is alive with emerging green star-like leaves of bluebells and tufts of honeysuckle bursting from the elbows of dead-looking stems.

Time passes slowly, while all around life is bursting forth at the seams. It happens so fast that within a few short weeks this wooded lane will be transformed into a lush green place that throbs and heaves, filling the senses with movement and dance. And yet it passes so slowly that all a human consciousness can register is the energy of busy rooks and stuttering staccato notes of chaffinches from within the thicket.

A blackbird exocets by, fast, direct, at head height down the middle of the ride. He curves round a corner past the clump of reed mace and screeches his arrival with such urgency that a magpie over in the fields is set off. The machine-gun repeat of this charismatic black and white bird mixes with the country chorus for a moment.

I rise to my feet, sling bag over shoulder, and tramp on as the rooks again have lift off to noisily circle and quarter as I disturb their fleeting peace. They will have all alighted once more well before I get to the metalled road, turn left, and follow my nose downhill then up again.

Jobs to do this Week

In the Greenhouse

- Sow Giant Single sunflower, Moss Curled parsley, Salad Bowl and Tiger lettuce, Wellington F1 and Evesham Special Brussels sprout.

- Pot on Tumbler and Gardener's Delight tomatoes.

- Weed pots where leaf mould has harboured seeds which are germinating.

On the Plot

- Pinch away side growth from autumn-sown broad beans to encourage a strong single stem.

- Plant First Early potatoes.

- Water Brown Turkey fig generously.

- Plant onion sets in prepared ground, Setton and Red Baron.

- Sow Early Wonder beetroot, White Gem parsnip, Guardsman spring onion, Armetis and Starca carrot.

- Water globe artichokes well.

- Keep new sowings watered if the weather is dry.

- Plant out Lobjoits Green Cos lettuces, Spitfire cabbages, F1 Market Express turnips.

In the Garden

March 4th Week

Spring Cleaning

With the time of year being where it is, Dirty Nails has been having a jolly good spring clean both around the garden and in his shed. Pots and buckets have accumulated by the water butt, lengths of stick require sorting, bundles of this-and-that need to find a place out of the way but still handy. Paths want sweeping, undug beds must be mulched and turned over.

The shed has been worked hard over the winter, both as a veg store and workshop. Dirty Nails has been creating surface space, clearing the floor, and putting away odds-and-ends. He likes to keep himself uncluttered as April beckons because there is much to do and he needs to be organised in order to fit it all in.

Back on the plot, he is always mindful not to be over-tidy. He considers anywhere that could potentially be populated by wildlife as an important part of the veg garden ecosystem. Growing food crops can be very controlling of the land. His planting plans include leaving space for both wild plants and creatures to express themselves within and around the cultivated area. By striking a good balance, Dirty Nails manages to harvest plenty of edibles whilst working with and amongst the nature he loves. He is a big advocate of brambles (tops for blackberries, plucked and eaten raw during autumnal foraging expeditions) and stinging nettles (delicious steamed like spinach, with tender tips available for picking now). The enchantment value of working a piece of land complete with wild corners and pockets is often underestimated, too. Dirty Nails is a firm believer in changing things for the better, and not just for the sake of it.

Second Early Spuds

Whilst thrilling to the opera of surrounding birdsong, and gazing with child-like wonder at the twinkling, shimmering surfaces of his ponds, alive with thousands of wriggling tadpoles, Dirty Nails has been planting his Second Early spuds this week. Popped in to a depth of 6 inches (15 cm), he plants at 15 inch (38 cm) intervals in rows 2 feet (60 cm) apart. His Second Early spud of choice is Kestrel. It is a handsome potato, sporting purplish patches on oval tubers. They will bake, mash, or boil straight from the ground in July, August, or September and will store easily until at least New Year if well looked after.

FROM DIRTY NAILS' JOURNAL
ALLOTMENT DISPUTE

There are as many different ways to garden as there are gardeners. An allotment field or site must accommodate these myriad methods and values. Down St James over Easter weekend we had a clash of cultures. All sides were left feeling wronged and got-at, misunderstood and very angry.

We have a good community down here. No association or hierarchy, just a collection of bods who tend their plots in different ways and for various reasons. Food is obvious but other things are available to allotmenteers be they fresh air, escape, exercise, peace and solace, or whatever. Some of us work like our bellies depend on it, although thankfully in this time and place they don't. Others like to take a more leisurely and relaxed stroll through the seasons.

The Town Council administers the paperwork, and we muddle through happily enough. The plots are at various stages of cultivation, only a couple neglected, and the edges dance with an assortment of hedgerow vegetation as the year passes by. We are not an especially fussy collection of gardeners in my observation. The brambly, nettley patches muck along cheek-by-jowl with fine tilth and neat borders.

Anyway, this dispute occurred on Good Friday. An allotment neighbour came on site with heavy machinery and a mate. They not only prepared one of their enormous plots with the turn of a key, shift of gears and control of wheel, but also laid waste to a corner of the communal bramble patch. They did so because they don't want it, but it is not theirs to tamper with. That was my line anyway, when I went down to calm frayed tempers.

Some people like the edges clean and tidy, the paths mown neat and short. The whole site 'is a bloody disgrace' (and this includes all the working plots, I was told). Apparently such an unkempt allotment field has never before been seen. Somehow I doubt it. But their attitude suggested a mentality that differs from that of most who potter the hours away down here.

Their wish to employ available machinery to grub and plough, to drain, ditch and irrigate revealed a glimpse of that particular rural attitude that loves to divide the town and country into 'them' and 'us'. The bogginess of the briar patch renders it unworkable without serious readjustment. Such obstacles mean nothing to those for whom a morning's bulldozing and earth-moving is part and parcel of a good day's work. That we, and that includes all of us who bend our backs in peaceful

ALLOTMENT DISPUTE
continued

productive meditation, have stated that we want this area kept as a wildlife haven gets interpreted as wishy-washy preservation from townies who don't understand 'country ways'.

And there we left it; mechanical versus manual, chemical versus organic, country versus town. In the politest possible manner (for we are all ultimately just tenant farmers) I suggested that maybe land elsewhere could be rented if the disapproval of our allotments was for real, and not to pass judgement on the honest toil and labours of others. Somewhat pacified, but rather indignantly, the lads got in their van and headed home for lunch.

Jobs to do this Week

In the Greenhouse

- Keep crops moist but not wet.

- Keep well ventilated.

- Sow Logo kohl rabi, Prinz and Giant Prague celeriac.

- Check over.

On the Plot

- Harvest Jerusalem artichokes.

- Hand weed asparagus bed.

- Dig up last of the salsify roots.

- Weed amongst winter onions and shallots.

- Sow Hamburg parsley, scorzonera, salsify.

- Plant Red Baron onion sets.

- Plant Second Early and Salad potatoes.

- Prepare a bed for shallots.

- Plant shallots.

- Potter, tidy and sort.

- Wash pots lying around in need of attention.

- Check over the plot with an eye to keeping it all under control.

In the Garden

March 5th Week

Tending Globe Artichokes

This week Dirty Nails has been giving his over-wintering globe artichokes some tender loving care. Having defeated the worst of the weather aided by a thick leaf and bracken mulch (horticultural fleece is fine, too), they are growing strongly again. With an ever-present ear towards the weather forecast, Dirty Nails has raked the frost-proof protection away and consigned it to his compost heap. He has also stripped off a number of tatty outside leaves that were browning or wilted. Each of these plants looks fresh and vibrant, sporting lush crowns of silvery-green leaves.

Planting Figs

Late March or April is an ideal time for planting fig trees. Dirty Nails has been doing just that this week, although for maximum fruit production it is not quite so simple as plonking a healthy young specimen in the soil and watering. If planted like that, figs are apt to throw out considerable growth of limbs and leaves but not a lot in the way of fruit. To concentrate the tree's energy into reproducing (fruiting), it is essential to restrict the root-run. Figs also relish plenty of warm sunshine to ripen the young fruit-bearing wood, so Dirty Nails is growing his as a fan-trained specimen basking against a south west-facing shed wall. Brown Turkey is an excellent variety which will produce succulent brownish-purple fruit ripening during August and September.

The planting-pit should ideally be 5 feet (1½ metres) long and 3 feet (90 cm) wide and deep. Because of the position of permanent paths on his veg plot, Dirty Nails has had to adjust his hole to make it longer and thinner. He has lined the pit bottom with two over-lapping layers of roof slates, and a further 6 inches (15 cm) of rubble to aid good drainage. The sides are lined with corrugated iron sheets, and the pit ends with thick wooden board-walks. While replacing the excavated soil, he has trodden it all down at regular intervals to make it firm and solid throughout.

The young fig, as always sourced from a reliable and knowledgeable nursery, should be planted in a hole large enough to accommodate the spread-out roots and deep enough to ensure that the soil level aligns with the soil mark on the stem. Having worked the growing medium in amongst the roots with his fingers, Dirty Nails treads it firm.

Figs are thirsty, especially in late spring and early summer, so need to be watered well during this time. For the first season after planting, fertilisers and manures should be avoided whilst the tree establishes itself.

FROM DIRTY NAILS' JOURNAL
CRACKING UP

Emergent grass creates a soft carpet of green on the arable where Cole Street meets St James' Common. By the tumbledown barn, clayey surface soil dries daily, contracting and cracking, a maze of enlarging fissures defining the fault lines, like a map gone crazy. Where I walked with wellies calf-deep in mud in the youth of this month, now I travel in shoes and gather barely a clod. It has been cold and dry for nigh on three weeks now, barely a drop of rain save a few fleeting, apologetic flutterings of snow a few days previous.

And still the trees suck up vast quantities of water to power their immense, god-like forms and functions, even now developing billions of leaves and flowers within loosening scaly buds. The pink dotted pimples on thorny twigs of hawthorn promise a magical display of scented blooms come May, a crucial source of sustenance for the busy horde of insects that will emerge, seemingly from nothing, and be on the wing at that time in the future.

We need rain to turn the mud back into a soft textured medium ideal for the house martins that will be using it for nest building soon. In a few short days, rooks will have hungry and demanding nestlings to feed. The fields, caked hard and unforgiving, will be of no use to them if they cannot thrust those great dagger-like, grub-catching beaks of theirs into the moist earth and extract essential food for youngsters.

Right now, the rookery by the prison is heaving with the breeding season in full swing, and great oaks that stud the pastoral hedges hereabouts carry their share of active nests too. But rooks don't lay eggs and raise their babies in spring for no reason. The ingredients of warmth, wetness, increasing light, and burgeoning life are intimately tied in to their breeding success. And they need water, that most important and precious commodity on which all life depends, conspicuous by its current absence, as the cracking fields and crispy husks of muck-spread farmyard manure on pasture up towards Foyle Hill testify.

Jobs to do this Week

In the Greenhouse

- Check over all crops.

- Keep water-butt filled manually if rainfall is in short supply.

- Sow Westland Winter kale.

- Pot on tomatoes (Tumbler, Britain's Breakfast, Early Pak 7, Gardener's Delight), Rucola Coltivata rocket, Greyhound cabbage, Great Lakes lettuce.

On the Plot

- Check over.

- If shoots are strong enough remove twigs from garlic beds (placed to keep off cats).

- Sow Berlicum and Nantes 2 carrot, Boltardy beetroot, French Breakfast radish.

- Erect poles for runner beans.

- Clear bracken and twigs from around the crowns of globe artichokes.

- Hand weed amongst brassicas.

- Weed couch grass from along plot edges and especially in vicinity of asparagus bed.

- Harvest last of the red cabbages and dig over this area.

- Tidy away unused sticks, poles, plastic and other oddments.

- Dig out the last scorzonera thongs.

- Clear away bracken mulch from autumn-sown broad beans (it makes excellent compost).

- Snip off any dead limbs from Brown Turkey fig.

- Collect hazel bean and pea sticks from the local countryside and store for future use.

- Remove spent kale plants to the compost heap. Smash their woody stems with a hammer first to aid the rotting process.

- Plant out Early Wonder beetroot.

- Hoe between rows of all onions and shallots.

- Prepare vacant ground for future sowings.

- Water all young fruit trees. If dry, give roots a thorough soaking.

- Water garlic, globe artichokes, shallots and spuds.

- Clear and compost Thousandhead kale.

March Veg on the Menu

Leaves and greens

Kale, Dwarf Green Curled
Kale, Pentland Brig
Kale, Thousandhead
Kale, Westland Winter
Purple sprouting broccoli
Red cabbage
Spud, Pink Fir Apple (store)
Stinging nettles
White sprouting broccoli

Roots, tubers & stems

Celeriac
Jerusalem artichoke
Parsnip
Salsify
Scorzonera
Swede

Salads

Corn salad
Lettuce, Lobjoits Green Cos
Winter purslane

Onion tribe

Garlic (store)
Leek
Onion (store)
Shallot (store)
Spring onion

In the Garden April 1st Week

Cabbages

Dirty Nails has been planting out his summer cabbages this week. He sowed seed of Greyhound and Spitfire F1 varieties during the second week of February in the greenhouse. The seedlings are now up to 6 inches (15 cm) tall, each showing a clean set of leaves, and are ready to go into a warm and sunny bed. All cabbages like rich soil, so Dirty Nails had previously worked in some well rotted manure. He places the seedlings in their pots in a row at 2 feet (60 cm) intervals. Working back along the row, one at a time, with a trowel he digs a hole large enough to accommodate the root ball and slightly on the deep side. These are filled with water and allowed to drain. Then, one at a time, he taps each young cabbage out of its pot and firms gently into the hole. He plants his charges deeper than they were growing in the pot, with soil covering the original set of leaves.

Slugs can be a menace at this time of year, so Dirty Nails scatters a proprietary slug-stop barrier around his newly planted brassicas to keep the marauding molluscs at bay. He never poisons them, however, because slugs and snails are an important food source for many of his wildlife allies in the garden. Lastly, to bring on the greens to a harvestable condition hopefully from late May, he places a clear plastic cloche over each one and holds it in place with stiff wire pegs.

There are cabbage varieties for all seasons. January King is a winter cabbage that produces good, solid heads from December 'til March. With a characteristic red tinge to their outer leaf edges, they will stand well throughout even the coldest weather. Dirty Nails has been starting off his Jan Kings this week by sowing the seeds individually into small pots of multipurpose compost. They are pinhead-sized, with a greyish or browny hue. In an effort to cultivate the strongest and healthiest plants, Dirty Nails empties the entire seed packet contents into the palm of one hand, and picks out the largest seeds with a pair of tweezers. He places these into the compost to a depth of ½ an inch (1½ cm) and moistens with a sprinkle of water. He will nurture them in the greenhouse until around the end of June, by which time they should be big and strong enough to be planted outside in their final positions.

FROM DIRTY NAILS' JOURNAL
IN THE LAMBING FIELDS

It is always full of drama in the lambing fields during April. I took the high path off Motcombe Hollow towards Thanes, skirting horsey pastures to cross a sunken brook that twinkled, babbling within the fold of almost vertical banks carpeted with over-mature dog's mercury. As mossy pasture rose steeply in front, I could hear the faint roar of building rush hour traffic just over the brow of the hangings mixed with chiff-chaffs, scolding great tits and sheep.

Straggly-coated ewes stood and watched as their youngsters gambolled and played on the slopes. The air was full with their plaintive, somewhat desperate, bleating. A pair of magpies observed from away a short distance, obvious and handsome, strutting boldly in their distinctive plumage with long tails flicking expectantly.

A tiny lamb buffeted its head against the wire fence with mum and sibling the other side, crying pitifully. She just stood while the youngsters called to each other. I stood and watched too, then got uphill of the ungulate tot and ushered it along the fence a bit, to a gateway. The response was immediate and emphatic. Troubled lamb found access via the open gate down the way, passed through and stood momentarily disorientated, before charging up the bank to the family fold.

Another larger lamb, number 2A, was the other side of the fence and trapped by the layout of the wire. Mother 2A and an even smaller, younger number were calling anxiously. I clambered over and spoke kindly to the confused youngster who backed against a tree trunk, looked confused, but would not respond. Mum, the other side, stamped a front foot and pierced me with a sheep-eyed glare.

Knowing and respecting these much abused animals, not believing them to be stupid and seeing that the ewe was not interested in playing games, I barged through the brambles, grabbed lamb 2A by the haunches and pulled the little fellow into my arms. There was virtually nothing to this one at all. The lightweight was lifted to a reassuring chest then placed on mother's side of the fence, all four feet on the ground. Mum was already walking away as the happy lamb ran to her side. She glanced back as I turned also and watched after a few strides. Babe was kneeling under her now obediently standing body and suckling with a passion, little tail wagging frantically in the warm sunshine.

Jobs to do this Week

In the Greenhouse

- Water crops, check over, wash pots.

- Sow tray, half each of Salad Bowl and Buttercrunch lettuces.

- Sow Feltham First Early peas in pots.

- Sow Patrick kohl rabi, Green Sprouting calabrese, F1 Market Express turnip.

- Sow kale (Pentland Brig, Thousandhead, Westland Winter and Dwarf Green Curled), Marner Gruwefi and January King cabbage, Late and Early purple sprouting broccoli, Yolo Wonder and Long Red Marconi pepper.

On the Plot

- Check over all areas.

- Plant out Rocula Coltivata rocket and Anouk lettuce.

- Plant a row of Fuseau Jerusalem artichokes.

- Pull up and compost spent white sprouting plants.

- Dig and clear the last of the current season's cropping Jerusalem artichokes.

- Hoe between onion sets with a bent kitchen knife for close control.

- Plant out Swiss chard, leaf beet, Greyhound cabbages (the last under bottle cloches).

- Water roots, asparagus and elephant garlic thoroughly.

In the Garden April 2nd Week

Maincrop Potatoes

Dirty Nails has planted the last of his potato crop this week. He pops in chitted tubers of his chosen Maincrop and Salad varieties to a depth of 6 inches (15 cm) at 15 inch (38 cm) intervals along the trenches he prepared and nourished some weeks ago. Maincrops appreciate a little more growing space than First and Second Earlies, so he has allowed a good 2½ feet (75 cm) between these rows. In many areas, Maincrop spuds are prone to catching 'blight'.

This is a fungal disease which can be especially damaging during a warm and wet summer. Brown blotches appear on the leaves, and within days the entire tops (or 'haulms') can die off. Dirty Nails is careful when choosing which Maincrop spud to cultivate, and always plumps for a modern variety bred with good or excellent blight resistance. He has dug a substantial harvest annually over the years thanks to a combination of good choice, good husbandry and good luck.

Ridge Cucumbers

In the greenhouse it is time to sow cucumber seeds. For Dirty Nails the variety of choice is Marketmore which is a reliable outdoor (or 'ridge') cucumber that likes to scramble up poles or netting. It produces prolifically throughout high-summer and into autumn. Scrumptious dark green, bitter-free fruits are much sought after by all the family. The creamy oval seeds resemble a large flattened grain of rice. Dirty Nails presses these into individual pots of fresh seed compost on edge, an inch (2½ cm) deep. After a little watering, he covers the pots with a pane of glass and some newspaper. When the seedlings start to emerge, he will remove the coverings. Dirty Nails avoids over-watering because cucumber seeds and seedlings are liable to rot if the growing medium is kept too wet.

The tender young individuals won't be planted outside until late-May or early-June, when frost is no longer a danger. In the meantime, a warm bed receiving full sun needs to be prepared. Ridge cucumbers do best with good heat up above and a warm root-run in rich soil down below. To ensure that they get at least some of what they want, Dirty Nails dumps one bucket of fresh manure at 2 feet (60 cm) intervals, with two buckets of good soil atop each mound. The cucumbers will be planted out onto these mounds, or 'ridges'. As for sunshine, when the time comes Dirty Nails will just have to keep his fingers crossed.

FROM DIRTY NAILS' JOURNAL
COPPICE STREET HEDGE

A tattered and shabby remnant of the old field system that was, but in places only just. Derelict through neglect, unkempt and thinning, growing out, pushed through, violated and dumped on. Small stretches are in quite good nick, layable if done within the next year or three. But mostly in need of a right old shake-up if it is to remain a viable hedge to present the living ancient face of Coppice Street and remind present day incumbents of their not so distant pastoral and linear woodland past.

Woody species abound: hawthorn, hazel, privet, elder, buckthorn, wych elm, field maple, mountain ash, English elm suckering up and dying back throughout. A habitat thick with sparrows that descend in small flocks to its protective bosom. Its greening skeletal form gives vantage to cock chaffinches with bright colours and greenfinches, whose gentle song sounds like dripping liquid gold. Down at heel, snuffle holes and latrines occur along its length as clues to nocturnal activities of badgers amongst the nettles and brambly thickets. It is a sad spectacle in need of some care lest some bright spark on a whim decides it is better, cleaner, cheaper, less rats-all-round to grub it out and erect a fence.

Yet despite the creeping degradation, Coppice Street hedge is a vital natural resource, a shrinking habitat that lives, dies and exists in our midst. With the bursting buds and calls of wild birds, this bustling hedge is demanding our attention.

Jobs to do this Week

In the Greenhouse

- Check seedlings.

- Sow True Gold sweetcorn, Goldrush and Yellow Straightneck courgette, Marketmore cucumber, squash (Uchiki Kuri, Butternut Waltham, Small Sugar and Spaghetti), Pure Luck okra.

On the Plot

- Hoe onions.

- Hand weed parsnips.

- Cut back encroaching vegetation at plot edges.

- Water all fruit and nut trees thoroughly.

- Plant Maincrop Picasso spuds.

- Water main crop onions, globe artichokes, roots, asparagus, shallots, garlic, broad beans.

- Hand weed strawberry barrels.

- Weed amongst roots.

- Thin scorzonera and Nantes 2 carrots.

- Sow Flamboyant radish, Purple Top Milan turnip, Logo kohl rabi, Buttercrunch lettuce.

In the Garden

April 3rd Week

Tending ... Strawberries

Dirty Nails has been planting out his strawberries this week. He sowed seeds of Alpine and Temptation F1 in early February and since then they have been developing a thick mass of roots and dainty crowns. He cultivates his Alpines in a shady, north-facing bed where they should thrive and fruit prolifically. Temptation F1 requires sunshine, and he grows these in an open position planted in rows at 8 inch (20 cm) intervals. He is hopeful that they will provide a small crop in the first season, and also throw out lots of baby plants on runners. He will tend these too, and pot them up in autumn to increase his stock. With luck, the original plants will harvest heavier in their second and third years.

... Kale

Kale sown in the first week of March has been potted on. The slugs have had their share of seedlings, even in the greenhouse, but many are untouched. Even now, the lovely crinkled edges of Pentland Brig and Westland Winter leaves are taking shape. Dirty Nails has moved them from 3½ inch (9 cm) to 5½ inch (14 cm) pots. Within a week they appear to have almost doubled in size. He pots them on deep, with the young greens buried firmly up to their first set of leaves.

... Carrots

Carrots can be patchy germinators. Some rows are showing pretty lines of delicate seedlings while others are sparse. Where germination has been poor, Dirty Nails re-sows with fresh seed. He simply makes a ½ inch (1 cm) deep groove with his finger along the lengths of row where no seedlings have appeared, sprinkles seeds into this, and brushes the soil over them with the back of his hand.

Where they have come up thick and consistent, early sowings can be thinned now. Dirty Nails loves getting in amongst his inch-high carrots. He selects the biggest and strongest seedlings to grow on, and carefully pulls out the others. Those left in the soil are firmed in gently. At this stage he aims to leave a single row of evenly spaced, slender-leaved plants. If they are an inch (2½ cm) apart that is fine, because they can gradually be thinned to larger spacings as they increase in size. All thinnings are put in a bucket and buried in the compost heap immediately, lest the dreaded Carrot Root Fly gets a sniff and a female descends to lay her eggs.

... Cucumbers

In the greenhouse, cucumber seeds sown last week have germinated with great gusto, so Dirty Nails has removed their newspaper and glass covering and is being very particular about keeping the soil moist but not wet.

FROM DIRTY NAILS' JOURNAL
SWALLOWS ABOVE
BATCOMBE RIDGE

Travelling between Lyons Gate and Evershot along that sinewy road that rides the ridge above Batcombe one morning in late April, my destination was the still distant Marshwood Vale. The drive offers a breathtaking contrast between bleak open arable and ancient woodland. Contorted figures of wizened oak and sycamore line the route. Expansive rolling fields to the left, and opposite down below a fairyland of classic pastoral, typically English patchwork quilted fields and copses as far as the eye can see. This is indeed a remote piece of country, although modern modes of travel bring everything closer and, as long as the machinery does not fail, it is nowadays only a short trip to almost anywhere.

Nonetheless, this quiet length of carriageway definitely demarks a change in both scenery and atmosphere. Maybe a muddy ancestral track was carved out along the chalky hilltop by folk who lived and died by the elemental forces. Forces which dominated their existences, ever-changing environmental moods which one day provide the landscape with a place in bright clear sunshine and the next see it cloaked in a shroud of mist and fog.

For the contemporary traveller, which includes me in a heated and comfortable smooth-riding motor, fortunately the magic of the place is still not lost. Taking five minutes to experience a snapshot of this essence on a warm and lovely spring morning, I pulled into a farm gateway, silenced the engine and sat in wonder as skylarks poured out a priceless stream of uplifting song from their tiny lungs somewhere high above.

But the real reason for stopping was to contemplate the sight of swallows drifting past in loose flocks of half a dozen or more. Unmistakeable and beautifully aerodynamic, darting little fellows in flashing blue, mesmerising because of the sheer incredibleness of the journey which they have undertaken only in the last week or so. From sub-Saharan Africa, with hippos and cheetahs, to mid-Dorset and beyond, with its rainforest-esque surge of April growth and bountiful supplies of insects. I cannot help but marvel at the enormous amount of unleashed energy which is all-enveloping, not yet half-way through the year.

Jobs to do this Week

In the Greenhouse

- Sow Limon borlotti beans, climbing French beans (Blauhilde, Cantare and Saxa), Streamline and Painted Lady runner beans, Haricot pole bean.

- Pot on early March sowings of Pentland Brig kale, Evesham Special and Wellington F1 Brussels sprout, Marner Gruwefi cabbage.

- Monitor seedlings daily and keep moist but not wet.

- Sow Long Tom aubergine, Giant Single sunflower.

- Pot on Tumbler and Gardener's Delight tomato.

On the Plot

- Check over all areas.

- Keep weeding any open ground earmarked for crops.

- Rub off unwanted buds on pear trees.

- Make sure you have time to pause and soak in the beauty of April.

- Plant out lettuces that are big and strong enough to cope with outdoor life.

- Sow rocket.

- Re-sow ungerminated lines of carrots.

- Plant out Greyhound and Spitfire cabbages.

- Plant up Early Pak 7 tomatoes in pots to go in a sunny sheltered place outdoors.

- Prick out or pot on January King cabbages and kale.

- Start to plant seedling leeks from trays into nursery beds.

- Thin carrots and beetroots.

- Keep on top of the weeds in the asparagus bed.

- Keep the hoe busy.

- Listen out for the first cuckoo of the year.

In the Garden

April 4th Week

Watching and Listening

As April transcends magically into May, Dirty Nails has the time of his life getting amongst his veg at every opportunity. As with children, tender loving care lavished at a young and formative age is a worthwhile investment for hopefully a healthy and productive life.

There is so much going on outdoors at this time of year that it is sometimes hard to keep track of it. Grass is growing visibly daily, leaves are bursting out and unfolding in a myriad of shapes and shades of green. Humming gently with busy bees, forget-me-nots and fairy ringers paint flower borders blue. Tulips provide bold splashes of temporary deep-purple and anenomies red.

For Dirty Nails, who is minded to get up at daybreak and bend his back for a couple of hours before work, the passing of late spring into early summer has multiple joys beyond tending shallots, lettuces, potatoes, and the like. Every morning he is treated to a chorus of male cuckoos calling across the valley that stretches out below his plot. Whether he pauses to stretch and drink in the hypnotic notes, or lends an ear while still scratching the ground, their music invokes some kind of religious experience in the listener, taking him to a place he wants to be.

Earlier in the week, before much of the motorised world had woken up in these parts, Dirty Nails was taking a breather, having a look around, thinking about something and nothing. Suddenly two roebuck crashed through the bramble thicket adjacent to his veg patch, one behind the other. They bounded along the path, over his spuds, and away through a gap in the hedge further up. Dirty Nails felt honoured to witness this snippet of their lives, was impressed by their handsome gracefulness, and aware that his unnoticed attendance at this scene meant nothing special to the deer. This chasing is typical roebuck behaviour at this time now, as they establish and defend territories.

Last evening just before dusk, Dirty Nails was watching gambolling lambs and their mothers in the next field. Like a slinky will-o-the-wisp, a fox appeared. He gave the newborns not a second glance as he trotted along, zig-zagging with his nose to the ground. The curve of the land took foxy out of sight for a few minutes, but his gingery, cat-like form came into view once more as he stole along a far hedge. Squatting twice to scent-mark tufts of grass, the fox came closer until he was sitting looking full on at Dirty Nails. Then, indiscernibly, the breeze must have changed direction because old 'Brother Dusty Feet' suddenly jumped up, turned tail, and dashed away into the encroaching gloom.

FROM DIRTY NAILS' JOURNAL
WATCHING BLACKCAPS
IN WEST DORSET

Have just spent over twenty mesmerising minutes listening to, and then watching, a male blackcap. His song is delicious, a rich and fulfilling warble delivered from amongst flowering pussy willow spilling out of the woodland just downstream from the main track bridge. The summer visitor's vibrant music was distinctive and beautiful over the chiffchaff's incessant repeat and the medley of other background birdsongs.

I walked over and stood, bathed in warm sunshine, looking into the shaded edge land for any sight or sign of movement. I scanned the area from which I believed the sound to come for ages, with many false alerts. Another blackcap even flew across the binocular-enhanced scene, momentarily distracting me from the chosen bird. Then, standing transfixed by the fluid-bodied bubbles and trills, I saw him taking to the wing and shifting position in the scrubby tangle to another sallow a bit further down. At last he was filling the lens, in full glorious real-life, flitting and skipping seamlessly amongst the yellow flowered scaffolding of twigs and branches. Then he stopped, opened his beak and poured out another cascading torrent of notes, feathers on his chest catching in a soft breeze.

I watched, knowing at that moment that this is what I had waited for. Indeed, this is why I had spent the money when I bought these binoculars many months ago! And spectacularly, another male came in to eye-shot. Another small bird with browny back, creamy-grey chest, nondescript looking and wearing a flat-cap of jet black feathers. 'My' bird continued to sing as the other moved on. Then, with a pause and a bob, he also took off. I dropped the glasses down and watched as he flew across the field corner and alighted in the brambles under some huge old ivy-clad oaks.

Jobs to do this Week

In the Greenhouse

- Tend and water seedlings.

- Set beer traps for slugs and snails.

- Pot on Green Curled parsley.

- Commence nightly torchlight expeditions into the greenhouse to seek out and evict slugs and snails.

On the Plot

- Hand weed here and there.

- Potter and tidy.

- Check over leeks in the nursery bed.

- Weed maincrop onions.

- Cut back or carefully strim plot edges.

- Hoe shallots.

- Hoe with care between rows of seedlings.

- Remove dead and brown leaves from purple sprouting broccoli.

- Use a rake to clear bracken mulch from broad beans.

- Weed the garlic and spuds.

- Hoe roots and main crop onions.

- Plant out Feltham First Early peas planted in early April.

April Veg on the Menu

Leaves and greens
Lovage
Purple sprouting broccoli
White sprouting broccoli

Roots, tubers & stems
Jerusalem artichoke
Radishes

Salads
Corn salad
Winter purslane

Onion tribe
Garlic (store)
Leek
Onion (store)

Edible flowers
Salsify

In the Garden May 1st Week

Earthing Up Spuds

Both First and Second Early spuds are up and showing, which pleases Dirty Nails. He grows his spuds in trenches with the excavated soil thrown up in ridges running adjacent. At this time in the season, the tops ('haulms') sprout at regular intervals from within the trench. His Concorde First Earlies, which were planted in mid-March, are most advanced. They have a rapidly-increasing tuft of healthy-looking greenery. Dirty Nails has earthed them up twice this week. It is a straightforward procedure which involves almost covering the haulms with fresh soil. This encourages further growth and more underground tuber production in the process.

These developing spuds need to be kept free from exposure to light, and earthing up does this job too. A draw (swan-necked) hoe is used to push and drag mounded soil from either side snugly around the haulms. Earthing up is an ongoing job as potatoes grow fast, and his Second Early Kestrel spuds will also need it done in the next day or two. Dirty Nails enjoys the look of freshly earthed-up tatties. Over the summer, his potato plot changes shape completely. The ridges and trenches gradually swap places until the entire bed is covered with dense foliage. Weeds are kept in check until then by the regular soil disturbance.

Greenhouse Slug Patrol

During a torchlight sortie in the greenhouse to remove feasting slugs and snails, Dirty Nails found a wonder of nature amongst his 4 to 6 inch (10 to 15 cm) high climbing French beans. Half concealed by the lush umbrella of green, shield-shaped seedling leaves, was a mass hatching of minute, pin-prick sized, yellow-and-black garden spiders. They had collected there, huddled together like a golden ball. In the beam of his torch the spider-bundle could be viewed close up, enmeshed within a complex matrix of glistening gossamer threads.

A few days later, the colony had relocated itself to the ceiling. The growing but still tiny spiderlings rested, suspended amongst an invisible web, until Dirty Nails accidentally jogged a line of attached strands amongst the beans. Thereupon the mass of dainty baby bodies exploded down and out like a miniature starburst, only regrouping slowly when the threat had passed.

Hand-picking destructive molluscs has proved very successful. Worryingly high numbers have been gathered up and re-homed into the wilderness beyond the back wall.

FROM DIRTY NAILS' JOURNAL
TESS'S STORY

Tess comes from East Dorset. As a tiny fox cub, she was found on a pig farm near Hurn. She lay, abandoned and lost, on a farm track. The farmer who found her at first mistook the little fox for a dead rat and carried on his duties. It was only later, when the farmer saw her move as he was passing, that she was taken in by this sympathetic soul.

Tess was initially raised in the farmhouse with cats, and they all rubbed along well. However, as is the case with most foxes in domestic situations, she grew too big and boisterous for the household. The farmer contacted an animal rescue worker in the New Forest, and Tess was moved to a new home.

The woman with whom she was now living noticed that Tess had been imprinted and preferred to spend her time in the company of humans as opposed to other foxes. She could not stay in the New Forest because of this. Another animal rescue worker paved the way for her passage to Walnut Tree Farm in West Dorset, the home of a couple called Derek and Elizabeth. Although they were both reticent at first, previous experience of raising wild mammals, and their compassionate disposition, meant that they were unable to turn the young vixen away. One spring, Tess arrived in the

Marshwood Vale in a small box.

A fox-release pen was already in position at a suitable location on the farm. It had belonged to a well-known wildlife photographer and author, and been used for many a year in his New Forest sanctuary at Amies Corner. At Walnut Tree Farm it had continued to help rehabilitate orphaned and injured foxes. Now it housed Tess.

After only two or three nights in her pen Tess was making it clear that she was significantly domesticated and craved human company. She was going frantic when left alone. This was very upsetting for her carers. Experts from around the country, with experience of foxes, were consulted. This was not a situation with which many people were familiar. No one was of the opinion that she could survive as a wild fox. Among the advice was the suggestion that Tess should be relocated to a sanctuary in Somerset where she could live out her life in captivity.

This was a tough time for Derek and Elizabeth. The responsibilities of taking on rescued wildlife are enormous and often thankless. Fortunately for Tess, she had ended up in the hands of a very special couple of people. Ignoring the suggestions and advice given, Derek and Elizabeth decided that she was to stay on the

TESS'S STORY

continued

farm. A close and powerful bond was developing between the species, and this was reinforced by time spent in each other's company. One day, Elizabeth let Tess out of her pen 'accidentally on purpose'. Amazingly, the fox trotted in and out while the door was open. At the end of that day Tess was shut into her pen.

When Elizabeth opened the pen door next day Tess shot out and vanished. For three nights she wasn't seen. Her carers became desperately worried about her. Surveillance cameras were rigged up to watch the pen, which had been left with the door ajar. Incredibly, the cameras picked up the image of a fox which was relayed to a television screen in the farmhouse. Was it Tess?

Next night, food was placed inside the pen and around the outside also. Elizabeth sat close by, calling in a voice which Tess should recognise. Seemingly out of nowhere, the little vixen burst out of the hedge, into Elizabeth's arms, and sat on her lap just like a pet cat. She was more interested in her human friend than the food, and showing all the signs of being very happy again.

Over the following nights, food was put out for Tess gradually nearer and nearer the farmhouse. Before long, she was feeding on the patio and sleeping in the conservatory as long as the door was never shut. She was living wild but using the farmhouse for food and shelter.

In that summer she was regularly attacked by resident foxes already living in the area. Tess would turn up at the farmhouse with various injuries, some of which were serious. She would unfailingly allow herself to be handled and treated by Derek and Elizabeth for wounds, cuts and chewed ears. Ointments applied

skilfully and patiently, tablets and tender loving care kept Tess as healthy as possible.

She was, and continued to be, a very emotional fox. Arriving at the farmhouse with fresh ailments, Tess would cry and whine until comforted by either of her special friends. After many months the bullying stopped. It appeared that Tess had established herself in this territory and was integrating well in the wild animal community.

Early last year Tess came up to the farmhouse as was her daily habit for food and grooming, except this time she was crying pitifully. As Elizabeth approached she ran off, then stopped a short distance away and turned around. Using this pattern of behaviour, Tess encouraged Elizabeth to follow her back to a fox earth in a hedge on the farm. It was a big earth, used for breeding. Tess went into the earth and Elizabeth waited, crouched at the entrance, talking gently and soothingly. Tess was sounding distressed, noisy and restless.

This behaviour was repeated again and again over the next few days. There was no sign of any cubs, but Tess's nipples did swell slightly. Derek and Elizabeth concluded that she had experienced some kind of phantom pregnancy.

This spring Tess has given birth to cubs of her own. She disappeared for three nights to bear her young and then recover. Since then, she has been busily raising them on whatever food she has been able to find, including increased rations from the farmhouse patio. Since giving birth, her visits have been noticeably brief and unfussy. The abandoned cub from Hurn has grown into a fully-functioning adult fox, and is now herself a mother.

Jobs to do this Week

In the Greenhouse

- Pot on kale (Dwarf Green Curled, Pentland Brig and Thousandhead), Early and Late purple sprouting broccoli, Marner Gruwefi and January King cabbage, Prinz celeriac.

- Nightly slug patrol.

- Keep refreshing beer traps.

- Sow calabrese and January King cabbages.

- Pot on Pure Luck okra, Salad Bowl lettuce, black knapweed (for the bees).

- Pot on cauliflowers very carefully, with minimal disturbance to roots.

On the Plot

- Prepare firm and fertile beds for kale and Brussels sprouts.

- Plant out Pentland Brig and Westland Wonder kale, Wellington F1 Brussels sprouts.

- Plant out Salad Bowl and Lobjoits Green Cos lettuce seedlings.

- Earth up First Early Concorde spuds.

- Sow Boltardy beetroot, White Lisbon spring onion, Berlicum and Autumn Giant carrots, Swiss chard, leaf beet.

- Pull up and compost purple sprouting broccoli plants.

- Start to clean, turn over and enrich a bed for this coming season's purple sprouting broccoli.

- Liquid feed tomatoes, broad beans, leaf beet.

- Plant out Marner Gruwefi Savoy cabbage.

- Keep leek nursery bed well watered.

- Erect poles ready for runner beans.

- Sow Best Of All swedes.

- Keep the hoe busy wherever and whenever possible.

- Plant out purple sprouting broccoli.

- Water all crops well if no rain is forthcoming.

- Thin carrot and lettuce seedlings (from a mid-April sowing).

- Check turnips for flea beetle damage and take preventative measures where it is severe. Light nibbling of leaves won't affect the crop.

- Earth up Second Early Kestrel spuds.

In the Garden

May 2nd Week

Planting Out Kale

In early March, Dirty Nails sowed kale seeds in pots in the greenhouse. The Pentland Brig and Westland Winter varieties have thrived and were transplanted into bigger pots mid-April. After a spell outside in the protection of a cold-frame, these strong young brassicas have been planted into their final growing positions this week. Their bed needs to be rich and well prepared. Dirty Nails weeds it completely, and firms hard by treading it down with small sideways footsteps, back and forth (the so-called 'gardener's shuffle'). He then rakes and treads some more.

Kale, like cabbages, Brussels sprouts and purple sprouting, needs really firm ground to anchor its roots and likes at least 2 feet (60 cm) between plants. Holes are dug with a trowel deep enough to take the kale up to its first set of leaves and filled with water. After allowing the water to drain, Dirty Nails pops the young plant in. As much growing medium is retained around the roots as possible. He uses his fingers to press soil down around the root ball. Then a boot heel is employed for a careful firming in, followed by another watering.

Cabbage Root Fly is a potential menace in early summer. The female will sniff out fresh plantings and lay her eggs in soil around the stems. When hatched, the grubs burrow down and feast on the roots which either kills or weakens the plant beyond repair. Dirty Nails thwarts the flies by fitting collars around the stems of all his brassicas

at planting-out time, which work as a physical barrier. He makes them out of carpet underlay, cut into 4 inch (10 cm) squares. A slit, with a little 'crow's foot' snipped at the end, allows a snug fly-proof fit for the cabbage root.

Pigeons can also be a problem. Dirty Nails ties strings between canes to criss-cross, creating a spider's web effect above his juicy plants. Coupled with take-away cartons dangling in the area too, this usually does the trick. Kale is remarkably tough and should grow on to produce fresh greens for winter.

Looking After Water Boatmen

The water butt is currently home to gangs of baby water boatmen, also known as 'back-swimmers'. Dirty Nails was alerted to their presence en masse when he took a bucket of water to decant off into smaller, more easily manageable portions for greenhouse use. As he dunked the can to fill up they used their long, paddle-shaped back legs like pairs of tiny oars to scatter and dive with a jerky urgency.

Although these pond dwelling insects travel from water-source to water-source by flying, he was concerned that sloshing them out of their chosen element indoors would not be good for them. This is an annual dilemma which Dirty Nails solves by using a fine-meshed sieve. He pours the butt water through this, which strains out the miniature black and silver boatmen. They can then be safely returned from whence they came.

FROM DIRTY NAILS' JOURNAL
CHRISTIES LANE IN MAY

The cow parsley that dances with frothy white flowers like a creamy mist on the banks of Christies Lane is a seasonal reminder of the sunken country byway that this once was. The wild garlic that forms a pungent bed beneath the elm thicket opposite, at the junction of Coppice Street, is likewise a throwback to a more rural, pastoral yesteryear. With houses and factories stretching deep into old fields that were, and a mystifying assortment of motorised vehicles travelling to and fro, small reminiscences such as these are a welcome relief from modernity.

An enormous sycamore grows on the far bank in a wooded belt, sentinel-like, dripping fresh palmate leaves that are almost luminous and catch the breeze and daylight to provide a lush and ever-changing kaleidoscope of green. Across the road opposite, an equally impressive monster beech. Thousands upon thousands of tiny lives pass between these two trees daily. If they could speak, tell a story of their time here, what secrets would they reveal? Of the muddy lane turned to metalled racetrack? Of the horse and cart to car?

New trees planted in the winter just gone give hope for a future where nature has a place alongside the trappings of human progress. Blackbirds pinking amongst freshly strimmed grass clippings lift the spirit, but the thrushes' song is drowned out by engine noise and the scent of garlic is lost amongst a poisonous cocktail of petroleum fumes.

Jobs to do this Week

In the Greenhouse

- Check over seedlings and developing crops.
- Nightly slug and snail patrol with a torch.

- Sow Butternut Waltham squash, Nine Star Perennial broccoli.
- Pot on peppers (Yolo Wonder, Long Red Marconi and Ring o' Fire).

On the Plot

- Check over the veg patch.
- Thin beetroot seedlings.
- Hoe open ground to keep it clean for seed sowing.
- Sow Romanesque Florence fennel, Anouk and Great Lakes lettuce, Nantes 2 carrots.
- Cut back plot edges.
- Apply organic fertiliser to soil around bean poles and hoe in as a preparation before planting.
- Strain off concentrated liquid nettle and comfrey juice from old wormery and decant into storage bottles.
- Keep leek nursery bed watered in dry weather.
- Sow peas.
- Clear away spent corn salad and winter purslane plants.
- Plant out Evesham Special Brussels sprouts.
- Keep swedes moist
- Water all potted veg and seedling crops.

- Sow White Lisbon spring onion, Amsterdam Forcing 3 carrot, Tom Thumb lettuce.
- Keep an eye and ear to the weather forecast; if frost threatens, earth up spuds in the daytime and sprinkle grass clippings on the green tips to give some protection from being nipped.
- Plant out January King cabbage, Brussels sprouts, Westland Winter and Thousandhead kale.
- Weed amongst main crop onions.
- Water well all roots.
- Sow French Breakfast radish.
- Sow spinach.
- Thin carrots.
- Keep weeding asparagus bed a little and often.
- Weed shallots.
- Plant out Cantare and Saxa dwarf French beans, Green Sprouting calabrese.
- Potter constructively.
- Cut back fruit bushes.

In the Garden May 3rd Week

Succession Sowing

Sowing seeds is so rewarding and fun at this time of year! Since the beginning of May, Dirty Nails has put down 6 foot (2 metre) rows of beetroot (Boltardy), Spring onion (White Lisbon), carrot (Berlicum and Autumn Giant), Swiss chard, leaf beet, lettuce (Anouk, Little Gem, Great Lakes), and Florence fennel (Romanesque). With two short weeks barely passed everything except the fennel is already showing. In fairness, it only went in a few days ago.

Suitable varieties of these crops and others were sown in the preceding two or three months. After a slow start they are coming on nicely. Dirty Nails has been close in amongst them, thinning out. This is a fine job to do on a calm, warm day. He selects the poorest and weakest seedlings in the line and pulls them out. This leaves only the strongest, biggest plants and they can be thinned again in due course allowing extra space for the others to fatten up. Some crops need more room than others so it is wise to consult the relevant seed packet.

What Dirty Nails sees when he casts an eye over the veg plot is a lot of foodstuffs coming on at different stages of development. This pleases him. Although seeds sown now grow amazingly quickly compared with the stuttery start of late winter/early spring sowings, they can't quite catch up. The result of this succession sowing is that there will be more veg in the kitchen over a longer period of time.

Bird Watching

One of the highlights of this gardening week for Dirty Nails was spending time on the veg plot with a friendly blackbird. The handsome fellow descended in sunshine shortly after the crops had been given a good watering. He hopped, skipped, and jumped right around the outside and then in amongst the rows, pausing regularly to cock his head and snatch a juicy tidbit.

This is a busy time of year for blackbirds, with a clutch of hungry mouths to feed back on the nest. Only when the blackbird emerged from a patch of nicely hearting iceberg lettuces, with his bright orange beak dripping full of wriggling worms, did he open his wings and take off over the hedge. Losing a parent now would be disastrous for chicks or fledglings, so Dirty Nails has a rule with cats in the garden. That is, whenever he is working in it they are politely but definitely shooed away. By doing so, the local birds have learnt when the coast is clear from cats for a safe visit.

FROM DIRTY NAILS' JOURNAL
ENJOYING PINE WALK

Pulling the foam plugs from my ears after wearing them for nigh-on two hours, I straightened and stood bathed in a shaft of sunlight. Dozens of birds immediately filled in with a cacophony of fluting warbles for what had been a continuous monotonous soundtrack of muted engine noise.

It is a lovely May day, warm, blue sky complete with high white, cotton wool cloud. Pine Walk is strimmed and blown, transformed from a jumble of spilling-over cow parsley and husks of beech buds on the deck to a cleaner, neater path that snakes away and undulates along its short length up, down and around corners.

Such is the intense depth and beauty of the trees and plants, the magic of the natural sounds, that walking this way on a day like this is almost psychedelic. Starting from St Johns Hill it is like a pine forest, becoming a lighter place that could be a Virginian mountain pass. Then into an English beech wood with monster trees towering skywards, like fantastic smooth grey elephants' legs, stretching up into their tender pale green canopies. Opening out up on Park Walk, and what could be finer? Mums pushing prams, couples kissing, family groups strolling gently. A barely discernable dance of heat haze shimmering just above the tarmac.

It is mid-afternoon; I have more to do. It does need to be noted, however, that right here right now, with St James down below and chaffinches all around, there is arguably no more agreeable place to be.

Jobs to do this Week

In the Greenhouse

- Put beans, cucurbits (courgettes, squashes and the like) and sweetcorn outside to harden off.

- Pot on sunflower, Giant Single, and place outside during the daytime to harden off.

- Sort, tidy and start to get the greenhouse ready to take tomatoes in grow bags.

- Plant Tumbler tomatoes into grow bags.

- Water and liquid feed tomatoes.

- Sort out cabbages and squashes for planting out.

On the Plot

- Plant out Dwarf Green Curled and Westland Winter kale, Painted Lady and Streamline runner bean, Haricot and Blauhilde climbing French bean, courgettes (Yellow Straightneck, Goldrush and Nero di Milano), Marner Gruwefi Savoy cabbage.

- Water spuds.

- Water seedlings and young crops.

- Select a range of healthy mixed specimens to give as early-summer gifts to friends.

- Hand weed leek nursery.

- Support broad beans with canes and string.

- Weed and hoe through rows of veg.

- Re-sow carrots if germination has been patchy.

- Earth up Kestrel Second Early spuds.

- Check over asparagus and cease cutting a young bed to boost strength for next year.

- Sow Saxa and Cantare dwarf French beans.

- Prepare a bed for purple sprouting by weeding, raking and treading firm.

- Earth up Maincrop and Salad potatoes.

- Plant out Early purple sprouting and the last of the kale.

- Gently and carefully train runner beans up their poles by tying loosely with soft string.

In the Garden

May 4th Week

Cucumbers

Dirty Nails has planted out his cucumbers this week. They are very sensitive creatures, especially when young. A cold snap in May can do damage so he waits as long as possible before getting them out into their final growing positions towards the end of the month. Dirty Nails cultivates Marketmore, which is a climbing outdoor (or 'ridge') variety producing an abundance of delicious, slightly spiky fruits. Having raised them from seed in the greenhouse (a windowsill is ideal, too) since mid-April, they are now sporting three or four lush, richly veined leaves, and look like they really want to get growing.

He prepared their bed some weeks ago. A sunny sight against a shed, with netting to clamber up, is ideal. The earth was enriched by heaping two buckets of soil onto one bucket of manure per plant, at 2 feet (60 cm) spacings. Dirty Nails only needed to part the top of each mound with his hands to accommodate the pot-grown cucumber root ball, fold the soil back and water in. He uses a fine rose on his can to sprinkle water lightly and gently from above.

Beans

Speaking of cold snaps, beans don't like them either. Dirty Nails has had lovingly nurtured runners and climbing French beans nipped and killed by frustrating mid-May frosts, and it is upsetting. However all is not lost, because beans can be sown direct into the ground now 1½ inches (4 cm) deep, at two seeds per cane to be thinned to the strongest. Although they won't crop until slightly later, steaming portions of lovely, tender green beans will be on the family menu this summer, all being well.

Feast and Fast

There are good years and bad for different veggies. Some years, a particular crop will grow like the clappers, while others won't shift for love nor money. It could be down to husbandry, weather, quality of seed, disease, pestilence, or the unexplained. For instance, leeks are generally a tough, reliable food source. Alas, a tray of Carentan 3 has been somewhat neglected which means that this year's pre-Christmas supply will be down on recent years.

Dirty Nails never tires of leeks, but this anticipated short fall is not the end of the world. In fact Mrs Nails is quite relieved, as she has confessed to becoming sick of the smell of them cooking towards the end of last winter. Hopefully the lack of leeks in the kitchen will be more than made up for by Ormskirk Savoy and January King cabbages. Both are performing very well at the moment and inviting the promise of a bigger crop than usual.

Apples

A selection of apple trees was planted in the New Year, as maiden whips. They have thrived, producing abundant leaves and good blossom. However it is important to allow apples to establish themselves for at least a couple of years before letting them take the strain of bearing fruit. Therefore Dirty Nails has pinched out the pea-sized embryo apples forming on his trees. He is also giving them a good weekly bucket of water each. Patience and control exerted by the grower now, with the saplings in their formative years, should hopefully result in stronger, healthier, heavier cropping trees in the future.

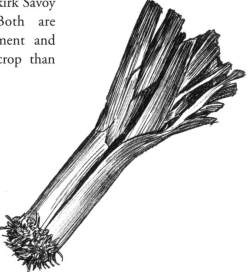

FROM DIRTY NAILS' JOURNAL
OF THE WOODS

I always take a gentle pace when going on down through the woods. This is not just because the deeply rutted, muddy, sloshing tracks demand it but because in here, amongst the giants that stand as living monuments, totally complex and incomprehensively marvellous as you or me in their own unique and individual ways, I feel compelled to just take time to stand and stare. Call it a fascination: maybe it is their incredible size, or perhaps the sweet music of woodland birds that envelops my senses and captures the soul for the period of time I allow myself to be lulled into this special place. To put my mind and body into neutral deep in Wincombe Woods is to lose track of that other world on top.

A world which began to change when I passed the Creamery and was confronted with the grandeur of unfettered hedgerow sycamores. When I stood sheltered beneath the canopy of one of these billowing sentinels and watched clouds of twittering, chattering house martins and swallows exploding from within and around the treetops, feasting on the seemingly limitless bounty of insect protein attracted into the vicinity of these tall trees, I was already somewhere else. The black and white martins twisted and curved in feeding-frenzied dance, swirling in response to the movement of their food and the buffeting of a pre-shower strengthening breeze. Swallows dashed and weaved lower down, jewels of flashing, streamered blue, trawling for morsels just above ground height like well-aimed pebbles skimming the surface of a pond.

And now, here is a place where five minutes passes into half an hour or more with effortless oblivion to timetables or appointments. The passage of what we describe as seconds, minutes, hours are but crude punctuation marks dreamt up by us to keep our lives in order. In the woods, long seasons and years count for what we might interpret as those tiny fractions of time to which we have wedded ourselves and are inextricably now enslaved throughout, if we are lucky, our 70-odd years or so.

This is a place where swirling winds over the top are calmed to a stroke, their roar hushed to a gentle purr that is scarcely noticed and certainly does not offend the ears. Where a shaft of sunlight can spear down between the trees and bring a bramble-skirted ride to glorious life, then ease away with such subtlety that its disappearance is only highlighted when the next blast of warming radiation makes you startle and think, 'Wow! The sun's out again!'

Of course, this environment is not here

OF THE WOODS
continued

without the hands of men. That these monster plants still stand hundreds of years after that small acorn or nugget of beech mast landed on the leaf-littered deck and got a toe-hold in the fertile woodland soil reflects the fact that no one has yet chosen to cut them down.

Even when I sit at home and look out of the rain-splashed window at the stair-rods lashing down, or have a cup of tea with my wife, or bend my back in the garden or on allotment, I need to know that these trees are here, as they have been for all that time, still doing whatever it is that they do as only they can. Knowledge of their continued existence orientates my spirit and sense of self, gives the locale a sense of place and belonging. They offer an opportunity to come along and share space and moments if the mood takes, regardless of whether or not that opportunity is embraced. By linking the past with the present and future their continuity is priceless, and all the more inspiring when viewed first-hand within hugging distance.

Even the stands of larches, planted with deliberation and choice, reverberating with the crisp trilling of warbling blackcaps and mirroring the blue carpet of bells beneath, strike a chord in my heart. Clumps of coppiced hazel, tall but dainty rowan adorned with thick creamy clusters of flowers and a canopy that sways and rocks in the wind, remind me that somewhere in the core of my being, in the distant instinctive memory of my ancestry, I am a woodland animal whose forebears came out of the trees and to whom the irresistible magic of this amazing world will be a powerful but at times almost tangible feeling, sense, emotion. Stuff that I must carry invisibly and take with me wherever I go.

Jobs to do this Week

In the Greenhouse

- Check over all crops.

- Water tomatoes daily.

- Pot on Green Sprouting calabrese sown in early May.

- Pot up French marigolds from the market into individual pots and place throughout the greenhouse to naturally deter blackfly.

- Pot on Black Beauty aubergine.

On the Plot

- Plant out marrow, Red (Uchiki) Kuri and Spaghetti squash.

- Weed amongst Jerusalem artichokes.

- Plant sunflowers in their final positions.

- Plant out Autumn Giant cauliflowers, celeriac, sweetcorn.

- Erect a barrier around the sweetcorn to deter badgers (who love the stuff!).

- Sort out accumulated rubbish.

- Take time to potter and absorb the early summer magic.

- Check over all crops.

- Weed amongst maincrop onions.

- Plant out Marketmore and Bush cucumbers.

- Water outdoor tomatoes.

- Sow lines of Autumn Giant carrot wherever space allows.

- Keep sweetcorn well watered.

- Earth up all spuds.

- If runner beans have been frostbitten sow fresh seeds (two per cane for later thinning to the strongest one).

- Replace courgette plants which may have been eaten by slugs with specimens purchased from the market.

- Hand weed here and there.

- Remove tiny developing apples from newly planted trees to conserve strength for future harvests.

- Keep the hoe busy between rows of veg.

- Clean and clear weeds from winter onion and shallot beds.

- Thin Swiss chard, leaf beet and lettuces.

- Take time on the plot with young relations, showing them the amazing things that happen. Get the nervous or inexperienced to do some watering, those with more confidence can get their hands dirty with some thinning or weeding.

- Thoroughly water young fruit trees.

May Veg on the Menu

Leaves and greens
Lovage
Purple sprouting broccoli

Roots, tubers & stems
Asparagus
Carrot thinnings
Radish
Rhubarb

Salads
Flat-leaved parsley
Lettuce, Anouk
Lettuce thinnings
Rocket
Winter purslane

Onion tribe
Chives
Leek
Onion (store)

Edible flowers
Salsify

In the Garden

June 1st Week

Sunshine & Showers, Weeds & Tomatoes

A few consecutive days of sunshine and showers can prove to be a heady mix in early June. There is a lush, dripping greenness to foliage which provides a perfect backdrop to the rainbow shades which flowers provide. In the orchard, they dance in anarchic swathes and patches. Their natural gay abandon contrasts and compliments the sumptuous, over-flowing, lovingly-tended shapes, colours and textures of the cottage garden. In the veg patch, Dirty Nails can admire the rich, deep browns and black of the wonderful, fertile, loamy soil that he is blessed to work with and maintain year on year with manure, leaf mould, and compost.

With growth taking on tropical rainforest proportions, Dirty Nails is happy to be able to eat some of the weeds that seem to be growing faster than anything else at this time of year. Smooth sow thistle is a common and prolific weed wherever humans disturb the land. Growing up to 3 feet (90 cm) or more, it has leaves that resemble those of the dandelion, but paler in colour, with a collared fringe where they join the stem. The edges are serrated, but not as angry-looking as its bolder, deeper-green relative the prickly sow thistle. When cut or snapped the hollow stem exudes a milky juice. Flowers resemble dandelion blooms, small yellow discs borne in bunches at the top of the plant.

The leaves make a nourishing, tasty alternative to spinach when cooked as such, but Dirty Nails likes it best when a few leaves are gathered and chopped finely for a cooling, mildly bitter addition to salad dressings. Sow thistles are reputed to have great restorative properties. Hunted hares, exhausted during the chase, were believed to rest up in the company of these plants and, having nibbled some leaves, were enlivened enough to escape their persecutors.

Dirty Nails is relieved to duck inside the greenhouse as another shower deluges. From there he can watch as water pours from gutters and water butts overflow. The richly red, veined leaves of beetroot and fabulous flowers adorning broad beans, make heartening viewing as rain batters down in rapidly dispersing circles on the roof.

Inside, tomatoes grown from seed are doing well. Dirty Nails planted up his grow-bags at the end of May, and not only have the plants shot up in size but they are laden with masses of the most delicate, yellow, star-like flowers. He is especially chuffed with the Tumbler variety. This is a prolific tomato, ideal for growing-bags and hanging baskets. It branches freely and there is no need for pinching out or removing any foliage, except that which is looking unhealthy.

Although plenty can go wrong between now and cropping, the signs are good for a bumper harvest. Every few days a splash of homemade nettle and comfrey tincture is mixed into a full watering can for a tomato feed. The greenhouse is decked out with a couple of dozen French marigolds, potted up individually. They appear to be succeeding in keeping the troublesome whitefly at bay.

63

FROM DIRTY NAILS' JOURNAL
SONG THRUSH

Nigh-on every morning since the mild turn of the year, on stumbling my early morning way up the garden path to unlock the shed and have a look around, I have been greeted by a musical songster of what I consider to be the highest calibre. A song thrush. Is it the same one or multiple individuals delighting my eardrums. I do not know for sure. But this bird, or these birds, perch in regular spots amongst elder and lime and sing out at regular times. More so also in the evening as the year has progressed. A series of notes repeated, a pause, then some more different tones, and it goes on. Squeaks, whistles, churrs, chimes – fluting beauty.

This morning it has rained from daybreak after a long spell of dryness and wind that had turned soil to dust on top. Thankfully not a deluge as so often happens these days, with big heavy drops descending like millions of hammer blows to beat down vegetation and cause flash-flood rivulets that scour the earth and wash away the powdery particles. No, an altogether friendlier rain of soft fine spots, enough to leave the greenhouse roof dripping intermittently and create a steady trickle of water from gutter to butt. As I stood sheltered in the greenhouse looking across the young orchard tucked, south-facing, under the hill, song thrush was on the path. He or she was looking for tidbits, with ruffled feathers fluffing up from time to time. A flutter up onto the logs, again to fence top, and away.

I fed my cat, spoke to wife and step-daughter, and readied myself for work. Once more to the shed. Thrush was high up on the ridged roof of the end-on cottages serenading the neighbourhood. Through binoculars I homed in close, leaning on the fence to steady my hands. Beak opening, the most elaborate fluid music was being sung with head thrown back and constantly turning, wind catching dampened feathers in untidy contrast to the lovely sounds.

Jobs to do this Week

In the Greenhouse

- Keep all crops watered daily.

- Pot on Pure Luck okra, peppers, Nine Star Perennial broccoli.

On the Plot

- Water beans, cucurbits, broad beans, Scrumptious apple, asparagus and onions.

- Spot-weed horsetail and bindweed from amongst onion bed.

- Cut back plot edges.

- Empty nettle-and-comfrey bin. Use pulp as a hearty mulch, decant and store remaining liquid, and refresh the bin with freshly cut nettle and comfrey leaves.

- Check over all crops.

- Give spuds a thorough drenching if conditions have been dry.

- Plant out January King cabbages, Green Sprouting calabrese.

- Earth up Second Early and Maincrop spuds.

- Thin lines of swedes.

- Keep podding and top-heavy broad beans well supported with canes and string.

- Cut back along the paths, sweep and keep clear.

In the Garden

June 2nd Week

Cylindra Beetroot

This week Dirty Nails has been making a final sowing of beetroot. At this time of year, he plumps for cultivating the Cylindra variety. It is a long-rooted beet, rich, deep purple in colour with a strong and distinctly earthy flavour. Beetroot sown now should, all being well, be ready for pulling in the autumn.

Dirty Nails rakes the seedbed to a fine tilth and marks out his rows with string tied between two canes. He allows a foot (30 cm) between rows, which gives the beets a chance to grow and swell unhindered. They could assume the proportions of a toilet-roll inner tube if the combination of sunshine and moisture is just right. A drill is made ½ an inch (1½ cm) deep with his finger, and into this Dirty Nails places the knobbly, irregular-shaped seeds at 1 inch (3 cm) intervals. When the seedlings are well up, and it won't be long, he will thin them to allow 5 inches (13 cm) between plants. These are generally a trouble-free veg to grow, requiring only to be kept moist and weed-free throughout high summer.

Long before the roots are ready, Dirty Nails will be selecting handsome, young, glossy beet leaves for a flavoursome addition to salads, or for light steaming as a hot accompaniment with potatoes. The roots are ideal for slicing.

Cylindra stores well for winter use when harvested before the first frost, laid sideways into boxes of dry sand or potting compost and kept cool and dark. Another way to enjoy beetroot out of season is to make it into delicious chutney.

FROM DIRTY NAILS' JOURNAL
WORKING FROM HOME

This is the summer weather that we have all been waiting for. Hot and high with a gently cooling breeze. Down White Hart Lane, almost opposite, jack-hammers are pounding a new smooth surface to slick over the bumpy hollowed dirt track that, until today, it was. I can hear a lump hammer being worked in a garden a few hedges and fences away. Insects hum and buzz. Jenny Wren stimulates an echoing chorus from somewhere in the undergrowth and crows waft lazy cartwheels in the sea of blue above.

Not yet eleven o'clock, I'm taking a breather. Having some time off is proving to be a healing holiday. With a wood pigeon directly overhead in the lime letting rip a gravelly, throaty delivery, swifts flashing across the roofs and side-winding above tree tops, starlings sitting atop a chimney chattering and clicking contentedly, this is a million miles from going to work.

In the greenhouse Tumbler tomatoes flop and loll out of their growing bags, festooned with delicate yellow star-like flowers curling at the ends to greet the sunshine, leaves scooping up like flat-fingered green hands reaching out as I brush past on my tending, watering, close-inspection rounds. Gardener's Delight are today tied in to canes. Clusters of embryonic buds promising a future worth waiting and living for.

Time ticks by relentlessly. Church clock bangs out top-of-the-hour chimes. I must get up from my idling on the greenhouse doorstep, cosied away at the back of the garden with my toms. Pussycat has just announced her sweet presence by tenderly climbing all over me for a rub and tickle, and is considering which shelf will afford the cosiest environs to curl up on. There is much to do apart from gardening: assignments, prep for meetings, articles to think about and other paperwork to knuckle down to. Being off the treadmill and not tied down for a few days gives me the freedom to duck into the shed, do a bit, come out and potter awhile or have a cup of tea and think, then get back to pen and paper. Far from being a chore, everything is a joy done this way. The only problem is that there are not enough hours in the day.

Jobs to do this Week

In the Greenhouse

- Check over and water crops daily.

- Tie tomatoes into supporting canes (not Tumblers).

- Liquid feed tomatoes.

On the Plot

- Thin Florence fennel, lettuces and carrots.

- Thin swedes.

- Hand weed asparagus bed.

- Check brassica plantings for signs of cabbage root fly. These will be pale and limp showing maggot-eaten roots crawling with white grubs. Remove entire cabbage to the fire site.

- Earth up spuds where needed.

- Keep paths and edges clean and tidy.

- Hand weed here and there.

- Tend runner beans by checking supports, providing water direct to the roots and removing all competing weeds.

- Keep the hoe busy.

- Potter, dream and admire!

- Weed thoroughly around globe artichokes and rhubarb.

- Sow Cylindra beetroot.

- Water brassicas, broad beans, squashes.

- Plant out Butternut and other squashes.

In the Garden June 3rd Week

Downy Mildew

Dirty Nails is suffering from an outbreak of downy mildew on his onions. Instead of being lush, erect and shiny, the green leaves have a dull, greyish hue and are dying back from the ends. His entire onion bed is infected, with most plants looking distinctly off-colour. Downy mildew is a potentially very damaging fungal infection which can strike at any time of the year, but the cool, damp conditions of a summer which is slow to start are ideal. The earlier in the season it strikes, the smaller the onions will be, plus they are unlikely to be much good for storing.

Dirty Nails is understandably very upset by this natural phenomenon, especially as there appears to be a secondary disease striking too, which is creating crispy brown patches on the leaves. However, that is the nature of gardening, and vegetable growing especially can seem like a constant battle with the forces of nature. Dirty Nails has removed all the infected foliage to a fire site, which has created a lot more room between the plants. He is hoping that sunshine now will radiate more freely amongst his crop and might slow down the attack. Nevertheless, downy mildew spreads its spores via water-splash from rain and on the breeze, so his hopes are not high.

Recourse to heavy-duty chemicals is one avenue of action for the grower thus infected but Dirty Nails prefers to take a more relaxed option. That is, even though the bulbs are small, to start eating the crop straight away. At least it won't be wasted, and the lack of home-produced onions this coming winter can be overcome by purchasing them from more fortunate growers instead. He plans to try again next season on a fresh site which has not grown onions, leeks, shallots, or garlic for at least two years.

A Much-needed Present

Mrs Nails recently gave her husband some reinforced waterproof knee-pads as a birthday present. Knees do a lot of work when gardening, and Dirty Nails is wondering how he ever managed without them. They make 'fine tuning' and fiddly jobs such as thinning seedlings or weeding close in amongst a standing crop far more comfortable. The position of a kneeling pad must be constantly adjusted, whereas strapped-on pads are there whenever weight is put on to those joints. With the novelty unlikely to wear off, Dirty Nails is looking forward to hours of fun scrambling about in the veg patch on all-fours.

FROM DIRTY NAILS' JOURNAL
MID-SUMMER IN ST JAMES

The finest show of elderflowers for many a summer illuminated the dusky hangings on Solstice eve, their platters of flowers like offerings handed out by the trees, rocked ever so gently from the warm breeze. Darkness quickened and a three-quarter moon lit up the sky like a silver sixpence being pushed through a slot. It had been one of the hottest days of the year, the humidity building for a day or two.

In the morning, the sun had broken open the haze and a big crystal-blue sky yawned wide enough to fit in everything. Plants in the greenhouse got heatstroke as their compost dried out. On the plot beetroot and spinach wilted at noon then revived in the evening. Swifts gathered in groups of up to a dozen, flew in squadron formation then exploded, scattering like celebratory black fireworks into screaming shards.

The longest day awoke hazily too, at about 4am. A thin shroud was soon burnt away. 7am now and it is hot, the sky clear and wispy clouds set up high, cast like a loose net. Down below birds unleash and flowers unfurl. Flies come in and out of earshot like tiny racing cars, a noisy in-your-face zigzagging. Chiffchaffs chiff and chaff plaintively from the wooded slope. A wren lets rip into mighty song from a rooftop aerial, continues the lung-burst in mid-flight, amazingly for one so

minute, and never pauses until the magnificent volley is finished.

In the border, a glamorous Italian version of Lords and Ladies has opened out its whorl of lush greenery to unsheathe a glistening, velvety-purple spike. It looks amazing, almost an exaggerated artist's impression of what it should be. But it really is like that, sexing up one corner of the garden next to a cattle trough full of green water, lily pads and frogs.

Jobs to do this Week

In the Greenhouse

- Water and liquid feed crops.
- Check over for signs of pests and disease.
- Keep well ventilated.

On the Plot

- Liquid feed for outdoor tomatoes.
- Cut off flowering shoots of rocket to encourage new fresh growth.
- Thin carrots.
- Tie in climbing beans.
- Generously water fruit trees and squashes.
- Tie in step-over apple trees to training wires.
- Stake tomato plants.
- Prune vine to within two leaf bracts of each grape bunch.

- Tie sunflowers to supporting canes.
- Second thinning for swedes.
- Hand weed and hoe Radar onion bed.
- Plant out Marathon calabrese.
- Remove and burn leaves from onions which are showing signs of downy mildew (looking mouldy).
- Sow Perfect 3 beetroot, Giant Winter spinach.
- Water generously wherever you can.

In the Garden June 4th Week

Red Cabbage

This week Dirty Nails has been sowing Red Drumhead cabbages. He favours starting them off in small pots of compost in the greenhouse but a finely raked seedbed outdoors is ideal too. He uses tweezers to pop the pinhead-sized, maroon-grey seeds in to a depth of ½ an inch (1½ cm), and keeps them warm and moist. When the seedlings are little more than 2 inches (5 cm) tall, they will be transplanted into bigger pots and placed outside.

If sown outdoors, seedlings should be thinned to allow 2 inches (5 cm) between plants before they are touching. Potted-on, Red Drumhead should suffer no ill-effects as long as the compost is kept moist and the roots are not constricted in their container. In four or five weeks, when the seedlings are about 6 inches (15 cm) in height, Dirty Nails will get them out into the veg plot. Direct sowings are best planted out into their final resting places at this stage too.

A site enriched for a previous crop is ideal, as these are hungry cabbages. Red Drumhead after broad beans is a good idea, because the recently-harvested bean haulms can simply be cut off at soil level and there is no need to turn the ground over. The nitrogen goodness in bean root nodules will be slow-released as they rot. Brassicas appreciate this.

All the cabbage tribe like to be planted out firm and deep. A trowel is used to dig planting holes allowing 2 feet (60 cm) each way. These will be filled with water and allowed to drain. After carefully planting the young beauties, and ensuring that there is no bare stem visible above the soil, Dirty Nails gently firms in with the heel of his boot. A horticultural fleece can be pegged over the cabbage patch at this time to keep white butterflies and other pests at bay.

Red Drumhead requires little else apart from being kept moist and free of weeds. Fleece can be removed come autumn when the weather cools, and the heads cut in wintertime. If they are being saved as a standing crop until spring, then a thick mulch of well-rotted manure can be applied around the stem bottom for nourishment after New Year.

This is a crisp and sweet red cabbage, traditionally pickled. It is also fabulous when steamed for a hot dish, but Dirty Nails grows it to make a quick and easy salad which all the family adore. A fat head is shredded with a sharp knife and into the mix is tossed raisins, balsamic vinegar, olive oil and seasoning to taste.

FROM DIRTY NAILS' JOURNAL
WATCHING A
DROWNING BEE RECOVER

Honey bees are inspiring insects. Half an hour ago one floated, spread-eagled and barely alive in a bucket of urine by the compost heap (collected for nightly spraying round the veggies, to try and keep the badgers from excessive digging). I fished the bee out with a twig and alighted the sorry fellow on the pallet edge of the compost in the sun. I then went down to my allotment to harvest broad beans, baby marrows and globe artichokes. On returning, I went to check on the bee. It was in the process of transforming itself from a sodden and unmoving article the size of my thumbnail into an amazing flying creature.

Every now and then, fending off black ants, the bee bucks and writhes, abdomen pulsating slightly all the while as legs are contorted at unlikely angles and the filth is combed away. The bee's body is dry and lightly furred once more. Its two black antennae feel gingerly in front of two huge multiple eyes. Bee crawls along the wood. With every burst of cleaning and drying effort it appears more healthy and active. Wings are still folded along its back until, as I look closely at my invertebrate friend and study it with wonder, they open and the bee has lift-off. It crash-lands next to my forearm. Seconds later, as the blazing sun yawns wide and hot from behind a massed bank of white and grey cloud, bee takes off again. This time, unfalteringly, the little worker buzzes off into the depths of Mrs Nails' flower garden.

Jobs to do this Week

In the Greenhouse

- Check over for signs of pests and disease.

- Water crops daily.

- Cut off discoloured lower leaves from tomato plants.

- Sow Red Drumhead and Pyramid F1 cabbage, Marathon F1 calabrese.

On the Plot

- Water cucumbers, sunflowers, runner beans, beetroot, squashes, kale and cabbages.

- Hoe through the cabbage patch.

- Water tomatoes in containers daily.

- Hand weed asparagus bed.

- Weed close in amongst climbing French beans.

- Clear ground for the receipt of maincrop leeks, and dibble these in.

- Snip tops off Witkiem broad beans to discourage blackfly. If these tender bits are clean, steam for delicious greens.

- Water newly planted leeks daily by 'puddling in'.

- Thin carrots.

June Veg on the Menu

Leaves and greens
Beetroot leaves (as spinach)
Leaf beet
Lovage
Stinging nettle
Sow thistle
Swiss chard

Roots, tubers & stems
Asparagus (mature bed only)
Beetroot
Carrot thinning
Kohl rabi
Radish

Salads
Florence fennel thinnings
Lettuce, Anouk
Lettuce thinnings
Rocket
Spuds, First Early Concorde

Onion tribe
Chives
Radar onion
Red Baron onion
Spring onions

Edible flowers
Globe artichoke
Salsify

Beans & peas
Broad bean, Aquadulce

Fruits
Alpine strawberry
Strawberry, Temptation F1

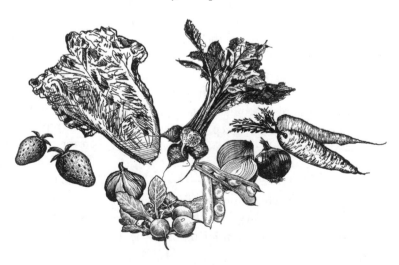

In the Garden July 1st Week

Harvesting Shallots

Shallots planted on the shortest day of the year are now ready for harvesting. Pulling ripe shallots is best done during dry and sunny weather. The tops are browning at their ends. Up to ten chestnut-sized, or larger, bulbs have miraculously been borne out of each individual set. Lifting the crop is both gentle and pleasurable. A fork is inserted diagonally beneath the cluster and levered up slightly to loosen the soil. Shallots sit on the surface. Dirty Nails takes hold of all the yellowing greenery on top and shakes the plants free of earth. When ripe, the multiple bulbs break apart easily in the hand, and he rubs off excess soil before putting them in a wheelbarrow.

Shallots store well. The crop will be tied into bunches of a dozen or so and hung in a cool, airy spot to dry off, until the tops have withered to a crunchy brown husk and the papery skins are crisp and flaky. An open-sided shed, or under eaves, is an ideal place. Dirty Nails will then remove any loose, dry exterior shell and keep them stacked in well ventilated vegetable trays. In the kitchen, Mrs Nails likes to simply peel whole shallots, place them on a flat tray, drizzle with olive oil, then roast until glistening and golden brown. Cooked thus, they have a deep, intense and rich flavour which gets the family's taste-buds drooling.

Potato Blight

Potato blight is a serious fungal infection which can strike anytime, anywhere. It is especially prevalent in warm, damp conditions. Spuds need to be regularly and thoroughly looked over throughout the growing season, with an extra-keen eye cast over the crop during thundery, humid spells in high-summer. Blight shows itself initially as brown blotches which appear at the sides and ends of leaves. Turn them over, and a fine ring of white fluff around the brown patches is visible in damp conditions. When left unchecked, the leaves and stems (haulm) quickly die back. If earthing up has failed to cover the tubers with sufficient soil then blight spores can infect the plant underground as well. This will ruin a crop, turning it into an unpleasant soft, wet, smelly mush.

Blight prevention measures include applying the copper-based 'Bordeaux mixture' via spray or watering-can following the manufacturer's instructions, avoiding the use of an overhead spray when watering, and patting smooth the earthed-up ridges with the back of a spade so that spores cannot easily be washed down into the soil. Once blight has taken hold, the only safe option is to remove the haulms altogether. Dirty Nails has been forced to do this with his blighted First Earlies. Although the crop will be reduced as a result, it won't be lost altogether. Second early and Maincrop varieties, although cultivated elsewhere on the plot, may not escape so lightly. Therefore Dirty Nails will be taking precautions by using Bordeaux mixture at the beginning and end of July, and once more mid-August at three weekly intervals, all the while holding his breath and keeping his fingers crossed.

FROM DIRTY NAILS' JOURNAL
TRINITY

Trinity is cut! Untouched since May 16th, the decommissioned churchyard was a meadow of seeded grass heads that danced like a heavy brown mist over the thick sward below. A sanctuary for bugs and yellow underwing moths, offering rich pickings for both insect eaters and seed feasters. And now it is tamed, brought back into the fold as it were, reclaimed from nature, where yesterday it was like a graveyard a hundred Julys ago. It has been strimmed and mowed into a beautiful subservience. Indomitable avenues of pollard limes stand proud on three sides. Their long shoots reach out across the path like dozens of thin-armed, green-fingered hands groping at the passers-by.

I sit, back to a tombstone that is encrusted with gold, black, grey and cream lichens. Blackbirds hop and skip amongst the drying hay, tossing it in all directions and swooping low across the open space. Greenfinches wheeze their lazy summer calls whilst hidden amongst the foliage with chirping sparrows, wrens and tits. Three clumps of ox-eye daisy stand out. Left untouched, they frolic with their guard of long grasses, facing the afternoon sun and absorbing the warm rays.

The limes seem to adopt a different character when they are in full leaf. They may be old, some are as rotten as a pear on the inside, and folk may see them as hard work and a liability to look after, but discerning wildlife-friendly eyes see them as haggard old giants that stand thick and hunched, as though simultaneously protecting and embodying the spirits that inhabit the Holy Trinity. Of course, such cosmic speculation may be just frivolous nonsense. They are simply lime trees after all, albeit managed by generations of people. They have assumed their present habits as a result. But nevertheless, as trees they may possess different kinds of magic known perhaps only by some beings and not others. Even if it is only to provide homes and atmosphere for fellow travellers, their standing is overlooked or ignored to the detriment of those who either cannot see or will not acknowledge.

Jobs to do this Week

In the Greenhouse

- Water crops daily.

- Liquid feed for tomatoes.

- Check tomatoes for signs of blight on foliage; remove any showing signs of discolouration and burn.

- Ventilate.

On the Plot

- Cut back vegetation overflowing onto paths.

- Keep plot edges clean and tidy.

- Harvest garlic and winter (Radar) onions.

- Water leeks every other day.

- Use stakes and string to support ferny asparagus tops and prevent wind damage.

- Start to train climbing cucumbers up their supports.

- Generously water fruit trees.

- Carefully weed amongst Cylindra beetroot seedlings.

- Strim paths.

- Water crops as needed.

- Thin winter spinach.

- Whenever signs of blight start to appear on spuds, don't delay; cut off and burn all top growth (haulm) immediately to check the swift spread of this disease.

- Thin Perfect 3 beetroot.

- Harvest shallots.

- Apply Bordeaux Mixture to healthy looking spuds.

- Sow White Lisbon and Ishikura spring onions.

In the Garden July 2nd Week

Harvesting Garlic

This week Dirty Nails has been digging up his garlic. Yellowing tops indicate ripening bulbs underground and are the cue for lifting. A fork is inserted to the full length of its tines (or prongs), and levered upwards to expose the aromatic bulbs. These can be laid out on dry ground in the sunshine for a week or two to completely ripen off, or tied in bunches of half a dozen or so plants and hung up in a covered airy place. Dirty Nails prefers to season his garlic this way because then he doesn't have to worry about whether or not it is going to rain. Also the sight of shallots, Radar onions and garlic hanging under his shed eaves pleases him enormously. They represent some of the first crops to be harvested and brought into store.

Working with Nature

Having staved off a blackfly attack on his spring-sown broad beans in early June by pinching out the tender growing tips, Dirty Nails is unconcerned by a return in force of the tiny sap-sucking insect pests. He will be taking no action against them for now. The broads have podded up nicely lower down, so no damage will be done to these. Allowing blackfly to remain on a crop where they can effect no harm is advantageous. Not only does it keep them off other susceptible veggies nearby but their natural enemies, such as ladybirds and lacewings, can have a good old feast and increase their numbers accordingly. This helps to maintain a well balanced predator/prey relationship in the garden.

Developing Froglets

In the pond, scenes of the most incredible natural wonder are taking place at this time of the year. Tiny froglets are massing around the edges and surface of the water, clambering over lily leaves and duckweed-encrusted stems of water mint and cress. Dirty Nails makes a point of keeping vegetation in the pond thick, and never has fish. He allows the surrounds to grow wild and untidy, providing lots of year-round cover. By having plenty of hidey-holes both within and without, and no goldfish to contend with, a high proportion of the frogspawn laid in early spring succeeds to develop into perfect miniature frogs no bigger than the size of a little finger nail.

The wildlife pond is thriving and is a fascinating place to watch closely. Alongside the froglets sitting still, perched on plant stems and leaves, or scrambling amongst the forest of growth in the cutest manner, less developed tadpoles swim to the surface. With back legs forming at the end of teardrop-shaped bodies, they take a gulp of air and then dive downwards with a lazy swish of the tail. Other taddies have four legs but their tails have not yet been reabsorbed. They wait in the shallows where water half covers unfurling lily pads.

The exodus has already begun, as Dirty Nails discovered when he chanced upon a froglet in a thick clump of grass sprouting like punky green hair at the base of his water butt. He cut the seeded heads off, then returned shears to the shed. Areas of long grass are vital to frogs in a neighbourhood of cats, rats and other predators. Allowing slightly unkempt places to remain is essential for the future survival of the gardener's amphibious friends.

FROM DIRTY NAILS' JOURNAL
MARBLED WHITES ON
WALNUT TREE FARM

With every step through the thick, wiry sward of myriad ripening grasses, clouds of butterflies rise in drifts from the path, dispersing like leaves caught in a gust of wind. They fritter away short distances, then tumble back into the seeded bosom to rest awhile. Mid-afternoon, the sun shines from a classic pale blue sky with scattered wisps of white clouds, motionless but ever-changing if you look away then glance back a few seconds later. A Marshwood breeze constantly strokes the grass tops, rustling amongst billowing hedgerows in tune with the rattle of umpteen thousand invisible grasshoppers. Forever-dripping notes of chiffchaffs and the echoing husky wheeze of woodpigeons lazily repeat from within the leafy copse. This is Walnut Tree Farm hay meadows in high-summer, days before the mid-July cut commences.

Gingery meadow browns and darker ringlets dance all around, and even as I stand still they are everywhere to be seen. From ankle height up to the hedge tops, dipping into the bramble flowers up there or the red clover down at heel, this is a living landscape that throbs and heaves as the whole of England must once have done, reverberating to the beat of tiny wings by the uncountable million, bringing the summer air to life with the vibrations created by their deceptively fragile patterns of flight, skipping and playing amongst bees and horseflies, one of which just landed on the back of my hand. With jaws like miniature pliers, it sank its vicious mouth-parts into my skin in an attack so stealthy, so silent and so painful that, despite the heat, it caused me to roll down my sleeves, tuck in and button up my shirt, and twitch violently at the slightest hint of an insect landing on my person.

I watched another through a hand lens. It landed on my trousers, vainly trying to get hold of the thick material. When observed in close up, the horsefly is an amazing looking insect, sporting brown and black marbling on its lozenge-shaped body and translucent wings. Such a handsome beast would surely be more lauded if it were benign, but this possessor of a painful bite is largely unloved. Working in their haunt, I fully appreciate why!

Where the creeping and marsh thistles are erect and flowering in patches around the field edge, their contorted stems are as tall as I am. They are topped with little barrel-shaped flasks and clusters of mauve and deep pink petals, twelve marbled whites on one plant alone in various marvellous poses. All busy about their business, the butterflies don't mind me as I stand

MARBLED WHITES ON
WALNUT TREE FARM
continued

in amazed fascination only a spit away. Rhythmically, they pulse open and shut their black-and-white chequered wings.

Like mini stained-glass windows the butterflies occasionally jostle for position, then settle again for more boozing through arching, straw-like tongues as long as their furry bodies. I can only stand and stare, having never seen anything like this before. Even as I wonder how to find the language which can properly convey this scene here and now onto paper, a constant stream of marbled whites dancing with others passes across my eyes, dropping in and out of vision as if to remind me that maybe this is one of those occasions when words alone are not enough.

Jobs to do this Week

In the Greenhouse

- Water crops daily.

- Liquid feed tomatoes.

- Keep tying in tomatoes to supporting canes.

- Keep well ventilated.

On the Plot

- Light hand weeding here and there as and when.

- Cut back plot edges.

- Cut nettles from around compost heaps.

- Cut comfrey leaves, allow to wilt in the sun, and apply as a mulch around runner beans or in rows between crops.

- Harvest elephant garlic.

- Water broad beans and kale.

- Keep water butts topped up in dry weather (use a hose).

- Plant out Nine Star Perennial broccoli.

- Plant out Giant Winter leeks into prepared ground.

- Stuff old wormery bin full with freshly cut nettles and comfrey.

- Puddle in newly planted leeks.

- Weed onions.

- Check over all crops.

- Remove any big weeds showing signs of flowering before seeds are set.

- Clear to compost bolted spinach plants.

- Liquid feed French and runner beans.

- Water courgettes and cucumbers.

- Weed around Jerusalem artichokes.

- Harvest shallots.

- Hoe amongst swedes and roots.

- Generously drench fruit trees.

- Harvest spring-sown garlic.

- Weed asparagus bed.

- Tie in step-over apples to training wires.

In the Garden

Tending Carrots

This week Dirty Nails has been tending his carrots. He has been weeding amongst the rows by hand and thinning his crop along the way. Those roots that are removed make a delicious and very flavoursome addition to stir-fries or salads. He is aiming for 5 inches (13 cm) or so between carrots by late summer, and gradually increases their spacings with each batch of thinnings taken out.

Carrots that have their shoulders exposed above the soil can develop a condition known as 'green top'. Although still edible, a green-topped carrot is unsightly and not the same as a lovely orange specimen. This problem is caused by too much exposure to sunlight. It is easily prevented by earthing up soil around the crowns in much the same way as one earths up potatoes, but on a smaller scale. Dirty Nails uses a hand-held swan-necked onion hoe to do the job. This action has the added bonus of helping to ward off carrot fly and suppress weeds.

Pruning Morello Cherry

This is an ideal time to prune a Morello cherry. Dirty Nails planted a sapling six months ago and is training his young tree as a herringbone fan against a north-facing shed wall. Selected branches are continually tied in to a framework of bamboo canes and wires to create the desired shape. He snips back with a sharp pair of secateurs any new growth that protrudes down or out. Morello cherries fruit on the previous year's growth, so within the framework this season's upward growing shoots are allowed to remain. They are tied to the canes with soft string as carefully as possible. These shoots should provide end-to-end blossom, and then cherries, next year. Older Morello cherries which are bearing fruit are best pruned immediately after harvesting.

FROM DIRTY NAILS' JOURNAL
ASH CLOSE

The thud and judder of heavy machinery provides a hectic backdrop for end of term 'Kwik Cricket', tennis and games at the all-change school, due for closure, re-fitting and reinvention. Houses have sprung up like urgent growth while the kids enjoy these halcyon days of summer before the big holiday.

The Eastern explosion of Shaftesbury is well under way as bricks and mortar replace blackthorn hedges and tender pasture. It will never be the same again. These youngsters are the check-out operators and trolley-pushers of the future, the shelf-fillers and edge-of-town dwellers of tomorrow. They'll not remember their town any different, except maybe in the distant haze of yesteryear.

The noise is movement, and the movements are increasing. Progress. But where does it go to? Bypasses, supermarkets, houses, industry, the sound of business being done. For now, stopping to lend an ear one can still hear the sparrows in the gardens, but they really are fainter today compared with a couple of weeks ago.

And then school is out. Exodus in all directions. Some have gone through a gap in the fence. In no time they have all dispersed. The digger grinds on. It looks like a violation, orange against the greens behind, resembles a dinosaur in the marshes, dipping for weeds with its long neck, gulping bucket-loads of earth and rubble.

Jobs to do this Week

In the Greenhouse

- Water crops.

- Check over and remove discoloured leaves (burn these).

- Liquid feed tomatoes and peppers.

- Put okra in pots outside in fine weather (daytime).

- Keep well ventilated.

On the Plot

- Tie shredded plastic bags to canes and insert the canes around Nine Star Perennial broccoli to keep off pigeons.

- Weed and water Cylindra beetroot.

- Weed amongst climbing beans.

- Water all crops in dry weather direct to the roots.

- Continue to 'puddle in' newly planted leeks.

- Do a bit of hoeing every time you visit the plot.

- Hand weed the asparagus; show the weeds no mercy in this area!

- Thin and earth up carrots.

- Prune and train Morello cherry.

- Cut back plot edges.

In the Garden July 4th Week

Salsify

Salsify is an easy vegetable to grow. Sandwich Island is Dirty Nails' preferred variety. It is equally at home in the veg patch, flower border, or anywhere in between. The half-inch (1½ cm) long thin, ridged seeds can be sown in spring and cultivated as a root veg to dig the following winter. Or it can be grown for its unopened flower buds. They are straightforward to harvest and cook, and taste remarkably like asparagus.

For an uncomplicated and mellow alternative to that much sought-after delicacy, Dirty Nails grows salsify in patches of up to a dozen plants in the orchard amongst his young fruit trees. Here they reliably produce more buds than the family can eat and also provide a beautiful display of purple, star-like flowers up to 3 feet (90 cm) high from late April until well into July. Insects love them too, and throughout high-summer swathes of delicate, fluffy brown seed heads open out to dry, like enlarged dandelion 'clocks'. This week Dirty Nails has been collecting the ripe seeds. They fall away from the end of the stem when enclosed in the palm of his hand and are laid out on newspaper in the shed to sort out and separate from their 'parachutes'.

For an exquisite asparagus-like experience in the future, he pops his seeds into small pots of moist compost an inch (2½ cm) deep during August, and nurtures them in partial sunlight for the rest of the summer. Dirty Nails over-winters these pot-grown individuals on a greenhouse shelf and will plant them outside into their final growing positions early the following spring. He allows 8 inch (20 cm) spacings at this stage. A few edible buds will likely be produced early in the summer, but serious indulgent pleasure is to be had in their second year. A decent sized patch of flowering salsify will throw up flower spikes in profusion for weeks on end, and self-seed freely.

The topper-most 5 inches (13 cm) of stem and bud is harvested by pinching off with thumbnail and first finger, whereupon a white milky juice which stains brown is exuded. In the kitchen Dirty Nails gives a generous bunch of buds a quick rinse before steaming them with a cupful of water for three or four minutes maximum, then serves up with a knob of vegetable margarine and a twist 'n' pinch of seasoning.

FROM DIRTY NAILS' JOURNAL
FROGLET EXODUS

It is amazing what a drop of rain can do. After weeks of virtually zero precipitation (since the first week of June) the town was treated to a drop or two yesterday afternoon. Warning signs were there, in the form of darkened clouds and a cooler, moist breeze. At 2 o'clock a gentle shower preceded a good downpour a couple hours later. Although it did rain real wet drops the duration was little more than ten minutes. Not enough to moisten more than surface vegetation and provide a tonic for the browning grass. But for some this lifeline was a trigger. The rain was enough to tempt assembling hordes of tiny froglets out of pond and into garden for a terrestrial adventure.

As I walked up the path and into veg patch, with overflowing fronds of courgettes and trailing cucumbers wetting my trousers from the knees down, and spade-like sunflower leaves brushing at my elbows and sides, this season's generation of surviving amphibious hoppers scattered across the ground like over-sized fleas. Although unable to claim any credit for their existence beyond providing their parents and themselves with a good home, the sight of their exodus gave me genuine paternal pangs. I have seen them grow from blobs of poker-dot jellied spawn, laid after a fifty-plus frog orgy in the early spring, watched their compelling progress with fascination and interest and charted their growth daily until now, when all corners of the garden seem to be venturing forth to eat and be eaten.

After a cup of tea and then continuing after dinner, I built a log pile shelter for the frogs against my shed. I planted pot-grown ox-eye daisy and knapweed around the pond and garden edges to grow large and lolling for future cover. With cats potentially in every direction, a wildlife-friendly plot must offer them as much sanctuary as is reasonably possible. And it is fun!

Jobs to do this Week

In the Greenhouse

- Water and tend.

- Liquid feed all crops once weekly.

- Keep greenhouse well ventilated.

On the Plot

- Keep up with targeted watering, especially of thirsty crops such as globe artichokes, brassicas, leeks, salads.

- Plant out purple sprouting.

- Compost exhausted and bolting 'cut-and-come-again' lettuces.

- Plant knapweed and ox-eye daisy in selected spots for the bees and other beneficial insects.

- Construct hidey-holes for the baby frogs which are leaving the ponds about now by piling logs in corners.

- Keep the hoe busy.

- Weed as you harvest to keep on top of the workload.

- Rake level bed where First Early potatoes were.

- Get in amongst the crops, hand weeding here and there.

- Spray Bordeaux mixture on Second Early and Maincrop spuds.

- Earth up sweetcorn.

- Collect salsify seeds to raise in pots or give to family and friends.

- Generously water young fruit trees.

In the Garden July 5th Week

Tomatoes

Ever since sowing tomato seeds way back during March, then planting them up in grow-bags in the greenhouse at the end of May, Dirty Nails has been carefully tending Gardener's Delight and Tumbler tomatoes. Each day he has given them water and thoroughly looked over his charges for signs of disease. Any discolouring leaves have been pinched off and burnt. Blight and other nasties have been kept at bay thus. *Botrytis* has not yet reared itself because the plants have not been overcrowded, and companion-planting with marigolds has so far warded off insect pests. His tomato plants are becoming laden with masses of fruit and the Tumblers are especially well-endowed.

Dirty Nails has now reduced the amount of water given to their roots. Instead of a daily soaking he is giving them a drink every two or three days only, depending on the heat and strength of the sun outside. He always stirs a drop of nettle and comfrey tincture into the water at this stage. Less frequent watering should stimulate his tomato plants' energy into fruit production and ripening instead of lots more foliage, which is what he wants to happen at this time of year.

Butterflies

Dirty Nails is a big fan of the butterfly bush, *Buddleia davidii*. He grows a few specimens around the veg plot to attract butterflies and many other insects. They flock to the nectar-rich flower cones. The purple-bloomed varieties are often on the turn as July gives way to August. By removing all the spent heads a second flowering flush can be induced. Done now, this may be timed to occur at the same time as many of the beautiful aristocratic butterflies such as peacock, red admiral, painted lady and small tortoiseshell are on the wing in large numbers.

Potatoes

Second Early spuds can be lifted with a reliable crop underneath any time around now. Dirty Nails only digs up what he needs for immediate use because if the tops (haulms) are still healthy then the tubers will be quite happy to stay where they are and fatten up some more. First Earlies have been on the menu for some weeks now but a request for baked potatoes from a visiting family member prompted Dirty Nails to harvest a clutch of Second Early Kestrel spuds this week. These are old-fashioned tasting tatties which usually come up a perfect size for baking and have a lovely fluffy texture. They also sport attractive purple patches on the skin. Care needs to be taken when harvesting spuds because they are easily skewered on carelessly placed fork prongs (tines).

Dirty Nails pulls away the haulm from the plant he is intent on eating, and removes this top-growth to the fire site. He then pushes in his fork parallel to the earthed-up row, slightly back from the bottom of the ridge and as deep as possible. The fork is levered upwards, exposing the tubers as he lifts the soil. This process is repeated several times for each plant in order to collect every last spud. It is unwise to overlook even the tiniest pea-sized tubers because they will sprout and grow next year. In that instance, being now of uncertified stock, these weed potatoes could become a vehicle for disease.

FROM DIRTY NAILS' JOURNAL
HAVING PICKED BEANS

Allotment number 16 is in its second uncultivated summer. It is an area of rank grass and hogweed umbels. Their scattered platters of flowers and ripening seed heads rise up three, four, five feet or more in a beautiful creamy-white swathe. Nearly 9 pm and all is peaceful down on the plot, save for occasional raucous laughter and voices from The Two Brewers, coughing sheep freshly sheared in the next door field, a football-rattling magpie, subdued swifts and a softly wheezing wood pigeon in the ivy-clad limbs of a hawthorn bush below.

In amongst the hogweed, which is adored by insects in spite of its blistering sap and bedevilled reputation, a patch of egg-yolk yellow ragwort spreads its massed daisy flowers, with globe artichokes gone wild standing thick and heavy, silvery-green. A clucking blackbird swoops in front. Satiated evening bees pass by. The clouds are a thick and heavy blanket up above.

The hilltop town hall clock strikes for the top of the hour. A couple of minutes later the church clock at the end of the street does likewise. Swifts get more vocal, another pigeon starts to chant. Fields towards Melbury are yellowing. Out across the vale the old weather-teller looks neither near nor far, giving no clues as to if the promised showers will come tomorrow. An assortment of beans fill my trug; French and runner. Time has come once more to bid farewell to this little patch of heaven, head up the path and homeward bound. Another day draws to a close. Exit is hastened by the cloud of biting midges that buzz ears and irritate my unusually un-hatted head. I have, as always, been on the plot for twice as long as anticipated.

Jobs to do this Week

In the Greenhouse

- Check over all crops.

- Reduce watering tomatoes to every other day with dilute liquid feed.

- Pot on Red Drumhead cabbages.

- Keep well ventilated.

On the Plot

- Allow savoured moments strolling around and looking over the veg patch with a keen eye; this is a great time of the year!

- Cut tops off Jerusalem artichokes to reduce wind damage in summer storms.

- Cut and remove seeded lovage stalks (save the seed).

- Clear the last of the broad beans but leave roots in the soil to rot down and release locked-up nitrogen for next crop.

- Stake fruit trees if deemed necessary.

- Hand weed here and there.

- Keep on top of invasive couch grass along plot edges. Remove and burn.

- Cut back all fruit bearing branches on vines to just beyond last bunch of grapes.

- Strim the paths and edges.

- Plant out Pyramid cabbages, Marathon F1 calabrese.

July Veg on the Menu

Leaves and greens
Cabbage, F1 Spitfire
Calabrese
Leaf beet
Spinach
Swiss chard

Roots, tubers & stems
Beetroot
Carrots
Florence fennel
Kohl rabi
Spud, Concorde
Spud, Kestrel
Turnip

Salads
Land cress
Lettuces

Onion tribe
Garlic
Radar onion (store)
Red onion
Shallot (store)
Spring onion

Edible flowers
Globe artichoke
Salsify

Beans & peas
Borlotti bean
Broad beans
Dwarf French beans, Saxa and Cantare
French bean, climbing
Peas
Runner beans
Okra

Vegetable Fruits
Baby marrow
Courgette
Cucumber, Bush
Marrow
Tomatoes

Fruits
Alpine strawberry
Black currant
Gooseberry
Strawberry, Temptation F1

In the Garden August 1st Week

Path Clearing

This week Dirty Nails has been out on the veg patch with his shears, hacking back the jungle of growth which was threatening to swallow up paths and access routes. Keeping walkways clear not only prevents Dirty Nails from getting a knee-down soaking whenever he ventures forth after a drop of rain, but it also acts as a seductive lure to tempt him up the garden path at every opportunity. He likes to keep a caretaker's eye on all his fruit and veg, and being distracted from seeing something important is all too easy when parts of the plot are being engulfed by the trailing fronds of self-sown nasturtiums or rampant cucurbits.

Lifting and Splitting Globe Artichokes

This is a good time of year to lift and split the crowns of three-year-old globe artichokes. At this age the plants have normally peaked in their production of delicious fist-sized flower heads, so Dirty Nails digs them up. It can be a strenuous job because the thick, dark brown roots are quite woody and go down a fair way. A garden spade is the ideal tool to employ, loosening all round to ensure a comfortable lift.

Fresh leaved grey-green side shoots (or chards) may be sprouting at the base of each crown. They should be treated with care; the same with any buds which are swelling in that area. These can be prized away from the bulk of the root mass with a sharp knife or pruning saw, retaining a chunk of root at the bottom of each and potted up in compost. With luck and careful tending, such off-cuts will provide the next three-year cycle of globe artichokes. Spent and unwanted stems and roots are very tough. They are best beaten to a pulp with a hammer before consigning to the compost heap.

For the remainder of the growing season Dirty Nails keeps his potted-up chards and buds moist and in as full sun as possible. They can over winter in an unheated greenhouse, porch or cold frame. He will plant them out in a new site the following March or April and keep fingers crossed for a reasonable crop in that first year.

FROM DIRTY NAILS' JOURNAL
TESS LOOKING GOOD
AND THE CUBS A-GROWING

She is a fantastic looking fox right now, lean and fit with a glossy coat that shines in the sunlight. A completely different appearance to the scrawny, tattered, exhausted little vixen of a few weeks ago. It is amazing to watch her interacting with Derek and Elizabeth, allowing herself to be cuddled, picked up and stroked. She gives every sign of actually wanting this attention, offering her belly for a tickle as a domestic cat or dog would. Frequently, when she is being fussed over, she will roll onto her feet and slink to just out of reach, then plonk herself down, look at her carer with what I can only describe as mischief in her eyes (ask any dog-owner about this trick, and they'll recognise this 'come on' glint in the eye), and flop down either fully stretched out or turned turtle again. She is quite happy to allow Elizabeth to closely inspect her teeth and coat.

As for food, this is supplied in abundance. Mainly chicken pieces, peanut butter sandwiches and fruit in the form of plums. Tess 'loads up', which involves her cramming as much grub as she can get in her mouth and is capable of carrying, then a bit more, and taking this off to the nearest far hedge. I watched her drop a morsel, and she stopped to glance back as if considering how to gather it up again. She was overloaded at this point anyway, so continued on to the hedge and out of sight. Tess reappeared soon after, minus food, and went to her dropped piece. This was buried in the long grass by scraping out a shallow hole with front paws, depositing the food, and covering it over by using her snout to smooth over a light covering of dusty soil and vegetation. She did a lot of this 'caching', which makes sense because if she is well fed so too are her cubs. She is storing surplus food for future, possibly leaner, times.

The cubs did not show themselves while I watched but Tess appeared to be taking some food to them still. For herself, she feasted on dog food which was gulped down on the patio. I departed for home with fox sprawled out on the grass by the patio in the beautiful evening sun. She was a bit nervous of me, sufficient for her not to want to be hand-fed a bit of chocolate (apparently her favourite!), but not enough to stop her usual routine. Watching this fox at close range with a quality pair of binoculars afforded me the most intimate sights I have ever been lucky enough to see in over 25 years of being an advocate for these wild dogs. It was an incredible experience. When Tess actually came into the conservatory where I was sitting I studied her with my naked eye. I was taken with just how small she really is, no bigger than an average sized cat.

Jobs to do this Week

In the Greenhouse

- Water and feed crops.

- Check daily for pests and diseases.

- Keep well ventilated.

- Pluck a few tomatoes at each visit to eat there and then. There is nothing like it!

On the Plot

- Formatively prune Oullin's Gage plum by nipping back all this year's shoots to 5 or 6 leaves. Remove prunings to the fire site.

- Water and feed tomatoes and other veggies in containers.

- Wash accumulating dirty pots which tend to litter the place.

- Start to thin grapes by snipping out tiniest ones from within the bunches.

- Plant Saxa dwarf French bean.

- Check over calabrese for caterpillars and eggs.

- Tie sunflowers to strong supports to prevent them keeling over under their own weight.

- Pick over all the cabbage tribe for cabbage white caterpillars and eggs.

- Weed amongst globe artichokes.

- Cut comfrey and top up the large plastic bin used to make nettle-and-comfrey tincture (liquid manure).

- Weed runner bean rows and cabbage patch.

- Dig up and split globe artichoke crowns. Pot up for the next generation.

- Water leeks and other crops as needed.

- Sow Enya lettuce in a tray, and put in a cool, partially shaded place to germinate (lettuce seeds fail in hot weather).

- Plant out Red Drumhead cabbages and cover new plantings with fleece.

In the Garden

Wildlife-friendly Strimming

Electric or petrol driven strimmers can be brilliant for knocking down tough undergrowth and cutting grass in awkward places. However, they are also lethal to frogs, slow worms and other creatures for whom rough edges and banks provide an otherwise safe haven. Dirty Nails is a regular strimmer user. Awareness of the damage they can do to small animals has caused him to think long and hard how to strim in a wildlife-friendly manner. Therefore he never strims where he cannot see, such as under bushes. Instead he will employ shears carefully whilst on his knees.

If close-mowing is not the order of the day, he strims to a height of 4 to 6 inches (10 to 15 cm). Where a tight cut is desired, Dirty Nails disturbs the area first by walking through it and then strimming backwards whenever possible. This flushes out any at-risk wildlife away from danger. Although it is easy to go into a trance-like state when strimming, he is conscious of remaining fully focussed and on frog-alert for the duration of the job.

Redcurrant Cordial-cum-presse

Having lost bumper crops of red currants to hungry birds over the last few years, a friend of Dirty Nails was minded to cover his bushes with netting this time around. It certainly did the trick and an enormous picking was had. A surplus trug of the plump, juicy beauties was happily swapped for some cucumbers this week, with instructions to 'Use 'em up quick!' Fortunately Mrs Nails was able to do just that. She produced a cordial-cum-presse of the finest quality.

Having roughly stripped the raw fruits from their stalks she rinsed them in cold water and laid them in a heavy pan. Fresh water was added to cover the berries, a lid placed on top, and this was brought to the boil. Mrs Nails used her intuition when adding two peeled lemons with sugar to taste, and simmered the brew for three-quarters of an hour. Once cooled, the contents of her pan were strained through muslin and funnelled into sterilised bottles. The resulting tincture was an absolutely delicious drink, intensely flavoured, rich in body, and a beautiful thick, deep-pink colour. Mrs Nails insisted that it was taken two parts juice to one part fizzy water for maximum refreshment.

FROM DIRTY NAILS' JOURNAL
SUMMER EVENING

Swifts are gathering up above the garden. A great swirling cloud of screaming, chirping, frantic wing-flapping, soaring, gliding, ducking-and-diving, muscle-strengthening feathered glory. Twenty, thirty, forty or more of them were just going crazy in tight-knit formation and have now loosened up, peppering the sky like dark tailed boomerangs.

An apple just fell, an inch or so across. You can be sure that even if no one was sitting close in quiet contemplation, it still would have made a sound.

The big old lime tree behind the veg patch is humming, literally, with bees. Either there is a swarming nest hidden within the leafy depths, or else neighbouring honeybees are working the flowers over-time.

No other sound. Nothing except swifts, bees and wood pigeons. They sit in the lime. Every now and then a big, fat, pink-breasted fellow swoops out and loops up with noisy flapping wings to the height he fancies, then holds his wings out and swings a line down that mirrors the lift. A slight turn upwards, more noisy flaps, another rise then fall, and he's back in the tree. Watching, preening, living his life this evening.

Mrs Nails is amongst the flowers. Watering can, secateurs, bucket. Footsteps, border fork and spade. The white buddleia planted some years previous has been wind-damaged and is too loose to survive. So out it comes, creating a new place to play with. She is going to try her luck with hollyhocks. I wish her success for I would love to see them each morning on my way up the garden path.

Jobs to do this Week

In the Greenhouse

- Water and feed all crops.

- Keep well ventilated.

- Remove diseased tomato leaves and stalks (burn, do not compost).

On the Plot

- Train branches of young Brown Turkey fig tree growing against the shed into a fan-shaped framework of bamboo canes.

- Plant out Red Drumhead cabbage.

- Water and feed crops in pots.

- Keep washing pots as and when to avoid having a mountain of cleaning to do in the autumn.

- Prune back step-over apple; side shoots to 4 or 5 leaves, tips back by a third.

- Feed and water calabrese and red cabbages.

- Keep young potted globe artichokes moist.

- Cut down and burn blighted Kestrel potato haulms.

- Do the same with Main crop (Picasso) and Salad (Pink Fir Apple) potatoes to save the crop. Leave tubers in the ground.

- Sow a tray of Salad Bowl lettuce; put in a cool shady place to germinate.

- Check over all crops.

- Take some time off to enjoy just watching and listening.

- Constantly check brassicas for caterpillar eggs under the leaves; rub out any patches or individuals with a thumb.

- Cut down all the Swiss chard and leaf beet to encourage fresh new tender growth.

- Cut back plot paths and edges.

- Keep the hoe busy in warm sunny weather.

In the Garden

August 3rd Week

China Rose Radishes

This week Dirty Nails has been planting radishes. At this time of year he plumps for cultivating the China Rose variety in short rows 6 inches (15 cm) apart. It is an excellent late summer and autumn radish. Roots can exceed 5 inches (12½ cm) in length and 2 inches (5 cm) in girth without any loss of quality to the crisp white flesh. China Rose can be succession-sown from June to September for a continual supply of hot and spicy pink-skinned portions. Later sowings can be lifted and stored in boxes of dry sand for consumption through the winter if desired.

When dealing with radishes Dirty Nails is always mindful that they are members of the cabbage tribe (brassicas) and avoids putting down repeated related crops in the same place. Having raked the weed-free soil to a fine tilth, he marks out the rows with string tied taught between two sticks. He then makes a ½ inch (2 cm) deep drill with his finger. The creamy-beige seeds are large enough to handle individually and he places them in the drill at 2 inch (5 cm) intervals. Soil is subsequently brushed over the top with the back of a hand. Before watering with a rose-ended can, Dirty Nails likes to gently tamp down the newly sown row with the flat end of a rake.

He will thin out the seedlings to about 5 inch (12½ cm) intervals well before there is any chance of overcrowding. This job is best done when the soil is damp and disturbance can be kept to a minimum. China Rose, in common with other radishes, favours a rich and finely textured soil that is soft. Moist but not wet is good. With plenty of warm sunshine as the essential added ingredient, Dirty Nails will be keeping his fingers crossed for a harvest in four to six weeks' time.

Cabbage Whites

There is an abundance of cabbage butterflies in the garden right now. Even though their caterpillars can ravage his purple sprouting and cabbages, Dirty Nails never tires of watching these dainty white beauties. On a sunny afternoon this week, as he and Mrs Nails nursed a cup of tea between jobs, they were treated to the spectacle of drifts of whites jigging in the canopies of surrounding trees, and descending on buddleia, verbena, nasturtium, calabrese and red cabbage. The fluttering, miniature clouds were everywhere, shifting positions like bubbles in a glass of lemonade. One group, weaving across the sky in close unison, looked like a dancing butterfly version of the Seven Sisters star constellation.

FROM DIRTY NAILS' JOURNAL
AMBULANCE STATION CAR PARK

Behind the ambulance station car park off Bimport there is an untidy jumble of thickety shrubbery that is in the process of being taken over by nature and reclaimed as a haunt for hoverflies, spiders and ivy. It backs onto the picturesque expanse of Castle Hill. Even to the most non-judgemental eye it is a mess. Not the sort of garden to welcome the inquisitive, but closer investigation reveals a certain magic and charm.

The enlarged trunks of elder bushes that have grown into trees are draped in a thick wrap of ivy. The cream-veined, evergreen-leaved creeper has spread its gripping stems all over the ground, engulfing and spilling over onto the tarmac on one side where tyres keep it in check occasionally, and on to grass on the other where regular mowing is a taming influence. In the middle of this would-be woodland, beams of sunlight filter through corky stems. At their tips, bunches of small green berries form intricate constellations. In the cool and still air hoverflies come in and out of view. Half a dozen of them fly in formation then disappear in different directions as if they were never there. These insects have a blink-and-you'll-miss-it style all of their own. Spiders sit and wait low down patiently, knowing that sooner or later dinner will be caught.

From underneath, flanking the deep and sweeping vale, the faint din of rush-hour traffic on the flyover is wafted up on rising air. Above, nestled in the thick canopy of a young but shapely sycamore, a wood pigeon purrs soft and throaty. Only the traveller who pauses beneath may sample the contented sighing. A perfect August day meanders past five o'clock with only a breeze to calm the oppressive heat of the previous two hours.

Jobs to do this Week

In the Greenhouse

- Water and feed all crops.

- Check over for pests and disease.

- Ventilate well.

- Sow winter purslane in a tray.

On the Plot

- Sow China Rose radish.

- Check calabrese and other brassicas for caterpillars and eggs.

- Keep the hoe busy everywhere.

- Pot up self sown butterfly bushes for planting at a later date.

- Cut and remove shading leaves from squashes and marrows to let sunlight onto fruits and encourage ripening.

- Liquid feed celeriac.

- Weed amongst leeks.

- Hand weed asparagus bed.

- Water and feed crops in pots.

- Keep plot and path edges tidy.

- Plant out Red Drumhead cabbages.

- Harvest Red Baron onions; lay them spread out on a wooden pallet in the sun to dry.

- Have a look at veggies under horticultural fleece for unseen signs of pests and disease.

In the Garden

August 4th Week

The Passing of Summer

The passing of summer was marked this week with hailstorms and some really nippy evenings. In the hedges and thickets, shiny blackberries are fat and overflowing. Elders hang heavy with the burden of their fruit and ripening plums dangle from drooping limbs, softening then splitting on the tree or falling to be gathered and plundered.

Above the garden, twittering flocks of twisting turning, zigging and zagging house martins assemble in dozens, with streamered swallows mixing in their midst. Robins, perched in an apple tree or atop the red berried hawthorn, clear their tiny throats, delicately showering Dirty Nails with their watery, sad-but-sweet music. Starlings tick and click, whirring and bubbling in small groups on rooftops and television aerials. Juveniles are losing their drab brown plumage and assuming a spangled, star-studded glossy coat which is as fabulous to look at through binoculars as their chattering is fascinating to lend an ear to for five minutes of rest and enjoyment.

Dragonflies quarter the garden, prehistoric relics who announce their presence via incredible bodies and wings that rustle in flight like paper fans. All around, amidst the hustle and bustle of man-made reality, older rhythms and movements are being danced. This is the season to feast, harvest and horde, as the nights draw in and 'October' is almost upon us.

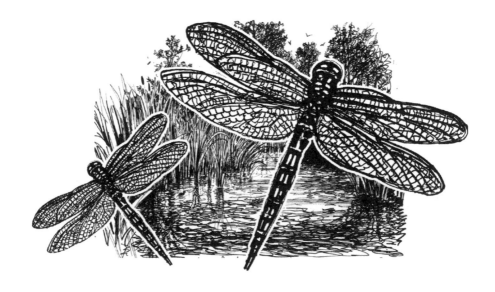

Harvesting Potatoes

Maincrop potatoes are ready for harvesting. Leaving them in the ground once the tops (haulms) have died down only increases the likelihood of slug or insect pest damage. This week Dirty Nails has been concentrating his energies on the big job ahead. He grows three varieties for autumn and winter use. Second Early Kestrel arc being lifted already on a dig-as-you-eat basis, and the remaining crop should see the family supplied until well into November. Maincrop spuds (this year he has grown the hopefully high-yielding, creamy textured Picasso variety) can be expected to keep in store for use after the Kestrels and beyond New Year. The Salad potato Pink Fir Apple is generally a good cropper and a long row of these knobbly, tubular tatties awaits attention too. They are good storers, to be used as and when the family fancies something deliciously different this winter.

A week or so prior to harvest time, the shrivelled tops are removed and burnt to avoid any chance of spreading disease. Baring the soil in this way hastens its drying, which is preferable when digging spuds. Wet soil is heavy to work and sticks to the lifted tubers.

Dirty Nails uses a potato fork for this task. It has ten prongs (tines) that are long and rounded at the end to prevent accidental skewering. They are shaped like a many-fingered shovel so as to cradle the crop of spuds when shaken free from the excavated sod. Being closely aligned they ensure that undersized specimens are not overlooked.

Dirty Nails likes to wash his spuds at this stage and is always careful when handling them. They are delicate and easily bruised. Damaged or unsound potatoes are no good for storing and put aside for immediate use. Ensuring adequate ventilation he sets the washed spuds out on layers of newspaper in the shed to dry. After a couple of days maximum, before exposure to the light turns them green and poisonous, he stores his potatoes one-deep in airy plastic fruit trays. These will go into a frost-free shed, the whole lot covered with thick cloth to maintain darkness at all times. The advantage of washing potatoes before storing becomes apparent on long chilly evenings when they are brought into the kitchen. There is no slopping about in cold buckets of water or blocking of sinks with mud before the all-important job of cooking can commence.

FROM DIRTY NAILS' JOURNAL
MISSING AN OLD MATE

I had a friend who I knew for fifteen years. I say 'had' because my old buddy is dead now, so it is all just memories. But when we were younger we were as thick as thieves. Many happy years we spent in close cahoots. But nothing lasts forever and our lives changed. He went there, did this and that, I went here and got on with other stuff. But through it all we'd come together annually just as though we'd never been apart. During those times we'd rub along just fine and dandy as good mates should.

In his later years, when I was settled and had put my roots down, he was still a wandering free-spirit and would come to stay from time to time. As the seasons came and went I could see his handsome good looks change as he got sicker. Although he became more belligerent his sparkling sense of fun and happiness that made him different from the rest was never lost.

My pal would come down south, park his rucksack full of bits wherever he fancied, and make himself at home in my house. His last couple of visits were in mid-summer. I would get in from work as tired as a baby lettuce from overdoing it in the sun and see the dinner table covered with shreds of tobacco, lighters and cigarette papers strewn all over, a pile of joints rolled and put to one side for the evening's consumption like a mini stack of cordwood. It was chaos for a few days.

The consistently late nights were not always what either Mrs Nails or I wanted but sooner or later he'd be gone, taking a box full of fresh veg with him: broad beans, beetroot, onions, potatoes and greens washed and ready to eat. I would heave an exhausted sigh. In fact we all would, and the kids would speak fondly of his habit of not wearing shoes and being constantly on the puff. We would sink back into comfy chairs and bliss out on the peace and undemanding quiet. Those were always great days, when the old Main Man would land on me to catch up and remember the good times.

Jobs to do this Week

In the Greenhouse

- Water and feed all crops.

- Keep well ventilated.

- Sort out tomatoes; prune off dead and diseased bits.

On the Plot

- Weed amongst spuds to get ground clean prior to lifting.

- Thin China Rose radish seedlings.

- Remove caterpillars from brassicas to sacrificial crops of nasturtiums cultivated for this purpose elsewhere.

- Put slates under ripening squashes and marrows to lift them clear of damp soil.

- Hand weed and hoe whenever and wherever you can.

- Compost early-season calabrese plants; bash the stalks with a hammer to aid swift decomposition.

- Check brassicas for butterfly eggs; with a thumb, smudge out any found.

- Tidy and sort the shed in preparation for storing veg.

- Sort and store previously harvested and dried garlic.

- Do the same with shallots.

- Harvest maincrop onions; lay out in the sun to dry or hang in an airy place in bunches.

- Tend celeriac by weeding and removing tough outer leaves.

- Prepare and pickle job-lots of cucumbers and onions if there is a glut.

- Commence the potato harvest by making a start on lifting Second Early Kestrels; wash them and leave to season and dry for a day or so then store in the dark.

In the Garden

August 5th Week

Caterpillar Plague

It has been a seasonably busy week for Dirty Nails. He is now paying the price for enjoying the spectacle of adult cabbage white butterflies rising and falling ten to the dozen over his brassicas in the dreamy haze of high-summer afternoons. Parts of the veg garden are now being overwhelmed by hundreds of chomping, twitching, insatiable-an-appetite caterpillars. The mottled black, green and yellow eating machines which are swarming over skeletal kale plants will become large whites. Less numerous leaf-green customers will change into small whites.

Caterpillar damage is often at its worst at this time of year. This is partly because one of the major predators of these pests, wasps, are no longer hunting them down in vast numbers. Throughout early and mid-summer wasps account for huge amounts of caterpillars which they feed to their grubs back in the nest. However, when the job of rearing young is completed in late summer wasps vacate the nest and disperse. They adopt a nomadic, scavenging lifestyle in which sweet sugary foods take a preference.

So Dirty Nails inspects his brassicas daily as part of his rounds. The kale should be tough enough to recover once a cold spell has taken its toll on the pesky pests, but Marathon F1 calabrese and Red Drumhead cabbage are altogether more highly bred and susceptible. Therefore, he has been relocating caterpillars into other places where he has deliberately grown nasturtiums as a sacrificial crop. Being a cultivator of wildlife as well as vegetables, the more effective and sensible option of squashing the offenders is not one which Dirty Nails chooses.

Potato Scab

The potato harvest is ongoing. Second Early Kestrel spuds have been dug this week. Dirty Nails finds this variety to be a reliable cropper which he grows on a fresh site every year. Some spuds have come up with rough brown pockmarks on the skin which tends to be in patches but is occasionally over the whole tuber. This is a condition called common scab which is no cause for concern. Scab is more prevalent in dry years. It only affects the appearance, not the cooking or eating qualities and can be simply removed by peeling.

Digging spuds is genuinely hard work but Dirty Nails loves it! Watching a forkful of soil crumble away to reveal a clutch of plump spuds is one of the finest moments of his vegetable growing year.

Bitter Cucumbers

Cucumbers are continuing to crop well. Dirty Nails cultivates Marketmore, a prolific outdoor ('ridge') variety that scrambles up netting on the sunny side of his shed. The fruits are perfect when about 6 inches (15 cm) in length, not too fat and easy to twist off the vine. At this stage they are at their cooling, watery zenith taste-wise. The occasional large 'cue' can be slightly bitter. If this is the case, Dirty Nails slices the top inch (2½ cm) off and rubs the cut surfaces together with a circular motion. Amazingly, a formerly bitter cucumber treated thus becomes completely palatable.

FROM DIRTY NAILS' JOURNAL
RAIN AFTER WORK

Home from work
Inside the old shed
With peeling paint on tin ceiling
And cobwebs in the corners
Alive with fat spiders.

Sitting with the cat
Who cleans herself daintily
Happy to have me home
At just gone five o'clock.

Light rain a-starting
Tip-tapping on the metalled roof
Not quite enough to fill the gutters yet

Although even now
As puss moves from the chair
Onto desk next to me
And continues to clean
Using her paw like a face-cloth
Whilst looking out dirty window
The drip-dropping begins
Of rainwater into the butt.

Time to put the pen down
And listen.

Jobs to do this Week

In the Greenhouse

- Water and feed crops.

- Pot on lettuces sown outside in trays during early August

- Engage in nightly slug and snail patrols with torchlight.

- Check for pests and diseases.

On the Plot

- Lift, wash, allow to dry, sort, rack and then stack spuds (in a cool, dark, well-ventilated place).

- Check brassicas for caterpillars and eggs.

- Water crops in pots.

- Harvest the largest marrows.

- Pull up and compost Florence fennel which has bolted (gone to seed).

August Veg on the Menu

Leaves and greens
Cabbage, January King
Calabrese
Leaf beet
Swiss chard

Roots, tubers & stems
Beetroot
Carrot
Florence fennel
Spud, Concorde
Spud, Kestrel

Salads
Land cress
Lettuces

Onion tribe
Garlic (store)
Onion (store)
Onion, Setton
Red onion
Shallot (store)
Spring onion

Beans, peas & pods
Borlotti bean
Chilli, Ring o' Fire
Dwarf French bean
French bean, climbing
Runner bean

Vegetable Fruits
Cucumber
Courgette
Marrow
Spaghetti squash
Squash
Tomato

Fruits
Apple, Scrumptious
Blackberries (from the wild as a treat)
Grapes
Strawberry, Temptation F1 and Alpine

In the Garden

September 1st Week

Cornelian Cherry Jam

This week Dirty Nails has been enjoying a jar of home-made Cornelian cherry jam, kindly given to him by old friends. The fruit-bearer grows in their front garden. Having recently moved into the property, his friends were thrilled to notice a heaving crop of oval-shaped shiny red berries up to ½ of an inch (2 cm) long adorning their small tree. A few weeks previous they were bright, tight and dry. At this time of year they have matured to a deep reddish purple and are so soft and ripe that the little stone in their centres can be popped out of the flesh by pressing it against the roof of mouth with tongue. The flesh is not insubstantial and has a mouth-watering, lingering flavour in between sweet and savoury. It may be accurately described as one of those 'special seasonal taste sensations'.

The Cornelian cherry (*Cornus mas*), or 'cornel', will flourish in most soils which are not acidic. A native of the European/Asian borderlands, it has been planted in the UK since at least the 16th century. It is ideal for smaller gardens and has ornamental as well as culinary benefits. The dogwood-type oval leaves are strongly veined, the bark is attractive, and pretty tufted yellow flowers are borne in clusters when the plant is still leafless in early spring. During former times the subsequent fruits were much prized for making preserves. It was this prospect which prompted creation of the gifted jam.

A simple made-up recipe resulted in three jars of a most unusual, rich, intense and very spreadable condiment. Having secured a large bowlful of the cherries through gentle shaking of the branches and careful ladder-work, Dirty Nails was told, they were pressed through a sieve to separate flesh from stone. Stones discarded, the resulting pulp was boosted with 1lb 10oz (¾ kg) of sugar and a whole lemon plus pips. The ingredients were slow-boiled for 'ages', with a few drops of water added in order to melt the sugar. When the consistency became jelly-like and too firm to pour off a spoon when cooled, the jam was ready to eat. With keeping qualities uncertain, Dirty Nails has been forced to consume a large daily ration. He does not mind a bit!

FROM DIRTY NAILS' JOURNAL
COMMUNAL RELAXATION
AMID REAL LIFE

The first batch of winter onions are in the ground, pressed down firm and snug in the shadow of a giant linden that punctuates the foot of the garden. It is alive with the football-rattle chatter of magpies, clucking blackbirds and rasping crows. Elders skirt the massive trunk with vigorous corky shoots and sprouts, which not two or three weeks ago were heavy with great dangling trusses of rich and plump berries. They now look tattier, picked clean in places by the flocks of thrushes and wood pigeons for whom such a feast is essential autumnal fare.

Cock bird now perches in the thicket with glossy black coat and bright orange beak, beady-eyed, quietly preening down his breast and under a wing. Meticulously grooming, taking a scaly foot to the back of the neck and scratching furiously. Then open wings and up, into the tangle of growth which fairly trembles with gentle morning activity from these fabulous songsters.

I sit on a wooden chair overlooking the newly-planted plot, bordered by leeks and a single-tier espalier Blenheim Orange apple, with my cat curled in a tight alert ball on my straight-backed and knees-together lap. She knows that the pleasure of communal relaxation is fleeting only. Cats learn the cycle of daytime rituals, just as wild creatures instinctively know what to do and when, in response to the inevitable and unstoppable seasonal ebb and flow. I must up and away in five short minutes to earn a crust, which sadly means that puss will be evicted and forced to seek another comfy spot to sleep off her breakfast.

Oh, to sit still another hour amid the collared doves and manic tits, to watch the teams of berry gulpers and thrill to the gigantic riposte of Jenny Wren as she tick-tacks along the fence top. Just as two grey-brown warblers corkscrew passed, twisting and turning in parallel flight almost within touching distance of each other, the time will come to remove myself from this real life scenario and go to work.

Jobs to do this Week

In the Greenhouse

- Water and feed crops.

- Remove spent French marigold plants to the compost.

- Keep well ventilated.

On the Plot

- Dig, wash, dry, sort and store spuds (damaged tubers should be put aside for immediate use).

- Check brassicas for caterpillars and remove if necessary.

- Keep the hoe busy wherever and whenever possible.

- Generously water young fruit trees.

- Prepare a bed for over-wintering Radar onions.

- Harvest sweetcorn.

- Apply water to the root zone of crops including celeriac and beans.

- Collect pot marigold and great mullein seeds when the weather is dry (store in a paper bag for next year).

- Plant Radar onion sets.

- Weed amongst globe artichoke crowns to keep perennial weeds at bay.

- Compost Florence fennel that has bolted.

- Compost exhausted Pure Luck okra plants.

In the Garden September 2nd Week

Quality Time in the Garden

This week Dirty Nails was pleased to be able to give away a marrow to his sister-in-law. These prolific vegetables are a favourite dish in her house. In the early autumn there is invariably a glut which needs to be eaten. A fine time was had by Dirty Nails and his nine-year old nephew who arrived late in the afternoon as arranged, armed with a freshly-sharpened knife. Together they cut the dark green mottled beast from a sprawling jungle of leaves and stems.

With the hard work done and dinner harvested, a mosey around the garden was essential. A great game was played which involved slicing marrow leaves into strips and spelling each other's name. It came as no surprise when, after the second round of this game, nephew announced that he had cut his finger and that it really hurt! Bravely and calmly the pastime was abandoned, a plaster located and applied to the wound with a gentle reassuring squeeze. All was well again.

Attention then turned to some inviting bunches of grapes. These hang in abundance from a vine trained up the side of a southwest facing shed and over a water butt. By mid-September they are at their ripe and juicy best, just perfect for eating. The bunches were taste-tested by plucking a couple of grapes from each. The yummiest bunch was selected and cut from the vine. Dirty Nails held it aloft and rotated it so that nephew could select the grape of his choice. They were declared the nicest grapes he had ever eaten, but what to do with the three pips located in each one?

Dirty Nails knew the answer. An hilarious game of pip-spitting ensued, both parties trying to get theirs as high up an 8 foot (2.4 metre) sunflower as possible. Although the veg patch is a working environment and not a playground, Dirty Nails is almost always happy to share the space with young nephews and neighbours. He can understand and relate to their wide-eyed wonder at the magic that surrounds them in the garden and feels honoured to be able to nurture a love and respect for the natural world in youngsters who are, after all, going to inherit the earth.

FROM DIRTY NAILS' JOURNAL
BADGER WATCHING

We sat there in wide-eyed amazement. Aged six, nine and thirty-seven, straining our ears to the whickering chatter of the rough-and-tumble of badgers as they gambolled down the slope of Pine Walk above and past Roger's Tree.

Huddled together as one, crouched in the yellow lamp-light at the top of Stoney Path. With a full moon watching over us to the south this was the pinnacle of our night walk, a 'Shaston dimension' which was coming to a chilly and tired end as we pondered our experience before descending the steeply cobbled hill.

As we did so, as quietly as we were able, a flash of white stripe caught the moonlit eye to our left in the garden of Jean and Ron, our neighbours. My uncle's protective grip tightened as I stood still and urged the boys to freeze with a quiet 'Shsssh'.

First one badger, then seconds later another, hurriedly crashed up the bank and scuttled across our path into the hedge at the foot of the lamp-post. The last to go stopped and checked us with a direct backwards stare, then bounded off into the shadowy darkness.

Jobs to do this Week

In the Greenhouse

- Water and feed crops as needed.

- Pot on lettuces.

- Ventilate.

On the Plot

- Cut back nettles and grasses around compost bins.

- Reduce height of Jerusalem artichokes by half.

- Clear spent courgette plants to the compost heap.

- Hack back encroaching brambles around plot edges.

- Dig, wash, dry, sort and store spuds.

- Tend Brussels sprouts by removing tatty, yellowing lower leaves and hoe in amongst.

- Water crops if the weather continues dry.

- De-caterpillar brassicas.

- Strim or mow paths. Trim the edges with shears.

- Earth up carrots.

- Hand weed as and when.

- Clean through parsnips, Hamburg parsley and other root crops.

In the Garden   September 3rd Week

Kale

This is a good time of year to tend kale and Dirty Nails has been doing just that this week. He uses a lump hammer to bash in stout metal rods at an outward angle next to his plants, which avoids damage to their roots, and then ties the stems to their new supports. This should help the roots to remain firm throughout any buffeting storms to come. A thick mulch of well-rotted manure is applied now too, which will give a nutritional boost and help the plants to recover speedily from the ravages of caterpillar and snail damage, which has been a problem in the previous few weeks.

Toads

Whilst digging the last of this year's potato crop, Dirty Nails chanced upon a couple of small toads. They had burrowed down into the ridged-up rows and were camouflaged with skin colouration which matched the soil exactly. With a diet of insects and small soil animals, toads do nothing but good in the garden and should be treated with the utmost respect. To this end, Dirty Nails cradled the slightly confused amphibians in the palm of his hand and allowed them time to collect their wits before relocating them in a rough patch behind his compost heap.

Toads only depend on water in the spring for breeding and outside of that season may be found in even very dry conditions. They differ from their frog cousins in that they prefer to walk and can only manage a feeble half hop, whereas bounding frogs literally leap along. Toads' skin is dry and distinctly warty. Frogs are smooth, moist, and show colour variances especially around the neck and legs.

Edible Gifts

It is easy to grow too much of any one vegetable and be faced with a glut. Knowing the right amount of a particular crop to cultivate so as not to be wasteful or sick of the sight of it comes with experience. Dirty Nails tries not to over-produce, and through meticulous planning, successional sowing and careful storing, is able to keep the kitchen supplied year-round with an interesting variety of veg which wants to be eaten.

However, there are times when the harvest is too plentiful. Runner beans in full swing can be prodigious and simply too much to cope with day after day. Courgettes have a habit of inundating the home producer with mini-marrows towards the end of summer. Giving away surplus veg is a friendly and neighbourly thing to do and affords Dirty Nails great pleasure; gifts such as a double handful of beans, the odd cucumber, globe artichokes in mid-summer, a clutch of freshly dug spuds, bundles of onions or the odd squash donated to youngsters for a Halloween lantern.

With his step-daughter leaving home and going to university this week, Dirty Nails was especially thrilled to be able to fill an old shoe box with an arrangement of home-grown veggies for her to take. It contained an uncomplicated assortment of spuds (including Pink Fir Apple, her favourite), red onions, shallots, garlic, squash, a punnet of tomatoes

and a bunch of grapes. Having been raised on this kind of fare, she knows how to deal with such basic ingredients in order to present an attractive and appetising meal. The hope is that eating these familiar foods in the first week or so after stepping out into the unknown will help her ease into the new life that lies ahead. And if, in the cooking, she pauses to remember her old step-dad bending his back on the plot through rain and shine, what more could he ask?

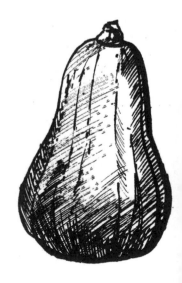

FROM DIRTY NAILS' JOURNAL
QUEEN MOTHER'S GARDEN

Raking leaves in the Queen Mother's Garden is a pleasure. Soft yellow lime leaves are each an individual delicacy in their own right. Tougher, crisper whitebeams, curled at their deepening edges. There's plenty of greenery up above, it is only mid-September after all. But the extreme dryness and heat of the summer has hastened the fall and here I am, collecting up the golden bounty, dreaming of leaf mould and digging.

It seems likely that this peaceful oasis is destined for conversion into a car park. Shame, methinks.

For now, one can still sit with back to a tree and gaze through tree trunks and shrubberies, birds and insects, shapes and forms, textures and colours. The beds at the front are a total mass of anarchic flower mayhem, vivid and alive. This place proves that the ordinary can be out of this world. There's a rose hedge at the front, laden with soft berries that look and feel like ripe cherry tomatoes. The hedge is a buffer from the noise and movement and fumes of the ceaseless traffic as it comes into town or through it via space-ship Ivy Cross. This is not a car park yet. It is still a living, breathing, ever-changing heavenly haven.

Jobs to do this Week

In the Greenhouse

- Compost leftover winter purslane and slug-damaged lettuce seedlings.

- If the weather is fine, put trays of green tomatoes on the shelves to ripen.

- Tidy up.

- Keep ventilated.

On the Plot

- Dig, wash, dry, grade and store main crop spuds.

- Weed amongst leeks.

- Gather grass clippings from whatever sources are available and add to the compost (do not use any that have been treated with chemicals).

- Spray brassicas with nettle tincture if caterpillar infestation is unmanageable.

- Construct new bins for leaf mould with wooden pallets lashed together using wire.

- Keep collecting and storing leaves from the autumn fall.

- Check over the leaves of curly kale for snails and slugs hiding away in the leaf folds.

- Generously water fig trees and vines.

- Keep the hoe busy all over.

- Water recently planted Radar onions. Firm back any which have lifted slightly.

- Harvest Uchiki Kuri squashes.

- Mulch Dwarf Green Curled kale with well rotted manure.

- Harvest Spaghetti squashes.

- Clean over ground recently cleared of crops and sow a green manure.

- Continue harvesting outdoor tomatoes, but burn plants which have finished cropping.

- Dig over vacant ground if it is heavy to allow natural forces of the weather to break it down to a crumbly tilth over the winter.

In the Garden   September 4th Week

Gathering Leaves

With the annual leaf fall in full swing once more, Dirty Nails has been busy collecting as much leaf litter as he can lay his hands on. Once they have had twelve months or so to transform into a soft and crumbly, sweet-smelling medium, leaves make a wonderful soil conditioner, either as a mulch or dug in. A simple way to make leaf mould (as decomposed leaves are known) is to stuff as many leaves as possible into plastic bags, tie them up, stab a few holes in the sides to allow the contents to breathe, and then store them somewhere out of the way until this time next year.

During dry spells leaves can be easily gathered with a lawn mower. Dirty Nails lifts the blades a couple or three notches higher than normal, then runs his mower over grassy areas inundated by fallen leaves with the collecting box on. Not only are they lifted with minimal effort, but they are also chopped up into shreds at the same time. This enables him to cram more raw product into the space available. Gathered thus, even tough leaves such as horse chestnut are sure to become a useful addition to the soil in a few months' time.

Watching Butterflies

Early one morning this week, as Dirty Nails stood by the back door before work, nursing a cup of tea and trying to decide what the weather might do, a bright object caught his eye high up in the canopy of next door's Bramley apple tree. It was the dazzling form of a red admiral butterfly which was sitting quite still, warming itself in the gentle rays of autumnal sunshine. Red admirals are handsome insects. Dirty Nails homed in on this individual through binoculars and was treated to a close-up view of its distinctive colouration.

The black wings arc up to 2½ inches (7 cm) across and each set shows a couple of fiery orange sashes top to bottom with splashes of white towards the tips. Tiny silvery half-moons punctuate the wing edges. As caterpillars they are nettle feeders. The gold-dotted chrysalis, which comes between the ugly duckling and beautiful white swan stages, may be seen hidden amongst the stems, where patches of this plant have been allowed to grow undisturbed in rough corners set aside for wildlife.

As September gives leave to October the adults like to feast on Michaelmas daisy, ice plant, and the juice from rotting fallen apples. Incidentally, Mrs Nails (who is in charge of flowers) succeeds in keeping her Michaelmas daisies to manageable proportions that don't straggle and flop all over the borders by snipping them back mid-season. She makes sure that her late season garden is well stocked with butterfly favourites which encourage some beautiful specimens to visit at this time of year.

FROM DIRTY NAILS' JOURNAL
STARLINGS

I pulled up to Wincombe Rec before noon in glorious autumnal sunshine. The sky was a clear deep azure-blue with the odd puff of cloud. Before getting out of my vehicle I watched through binoculars the antics of a 150-strong flock of grounded starlings. These quirky, happy little fellows, resplendent in their spangled shiny dark poker-dot plumage were having a fine old time feasting on crane flies. The gangly insects are hatching right now in their thousands, emerging from within the former pastures to bumble and clamber their incongruous way into the open to find a mate and reproduce.

In the stillness of the morning, to a background of cheeping sparrows and light aircraft high up overhead, the starlings were dashing back and forth, bright eyes keen and sharp, wide-open beaks thrust out in front to gobble up a tangle of juicy body and long, awkward legs. Pied wagtails picked their jaunty way along as a loose group of a dozen. The odd marauding, frisky crow stole in to rob discarded pastry and uneaten human fare from the smaller, browner youngsters. Amplified through field glasses, the view was magical and fascinating, not dissimilar from TV images of massed wildlife assemblies on the African plains or herds of Arctic tundra caribou.

The feeding frenzy continued in this fashion, with birds running hither and thither, until a Sunday stroller entered through the hinged wooden gate. They lifted as a rippled curve of over-taking and swirling bodies, alighting again as a flock on the other side of the field.

Jobs to do this Week

In the Greenhouse

- Clear out and burn spent aubergine plants.

- Start to do the same with tomato plants.

- Dismantle shelving in preparation for cleaning and disinfecting.

- Sort dirty pots for washing.

- Completely clear out and sweep.

- Ventilate.

On the Plot

- Collect leaves from outside sources and keep safely for future use.

- Prune step-over apple trees.

- Harvest Butternut squashes and marrows before the first frosts.

- Hand weed asparagus bed.

- Weed swedes.

- Turn over cleared ground.

- Clear and sweep paths. Now is a good time to make adjustments and/or widen if desired.

- Stake Nine Star Perennial broccoli against the wind.

- Repair broken panes of glass in the shed.

- Construct log piles in uncultivated corners to provide shelter for hibernating frogs and toads.

- Carry on weeding.

September Veg on the Menu

Leaves and greens
Calabrese, Marathon F1
Cauliflower
Leaf beet
Purple sprouting (bolted early and out of season)

Roots, tubers & stems
Beetroot
Carrot, Nantes 2
Celeriac
Spud, Kestrel
Spud, Picasso
Spuds, Pink Fir Apple

Salads
Lettuces

Onion tribe
Elephant garlic
Garlic (store)
Onion (store)
Red onion (store)
Shallot (store)
Spring onion

Beans, peas & pods
Borlotti beans
Chilli pepper
Dwarf French beans
French beans, climbing
Green pepper
Runner beans

Vegetable Fruits
Aubergine
Courgette
Cucumber
Marrow
Squash
Sweetcorn
Tomato

Fruits
Apple, Scrumptious
Grapes
Strawberry

In the Garden
October 1st Week

Bindweed & Horsetail

This week Dirty Nails has been busy turning over bits and pieces of open ground on his plot where areas have been vacated by harvested crops. He likes to do this sooner rather than later as it not only pleases his eye when leaning on a spade and contemplating the work ahead, but also keeps on top of the weeds. Dirty Nails tries to be meticulous in this department. Removing unwanted invaders before they have a chance to set seed or send down long tap roots saves much time and backache in the long run.

Ruderals are flowers such as speedwell, chickweed and shepherd's purse which evolved to complete their reproductive lifespan in a matter of weeks. They can quickly smother cleared areas. Having said that, at this time of year weed growth is noticeably slower than in the preceding few months. This can make weeding a rather mellow, peaceful, relaxing affair.

Two of the most troublesome species in his veg patch, which thankfully infest only parts of it and not the whole space, are bindweed (also known as convolvulus) and horsetail. They are perennials, coming up year after year from the same rootstock. Bindweed is a persistent strangling nuisance amongst crops. It sends out tough shoots that twist and coil anti-clockwise, latching onto the first thing they come into contact with. Underground, brittle white roots are hungry and extensive. Dirty Nails takes the time and trouble to dig deep, extracting every last piece, as even a tiny segment of root will quickly establish a new plant and become a problem in the wrong place.

Horsetail has been growing virtually unchanged as a species since the time of the dinosaurs. It flourishes in moist soils and waste ground. Undisturbed, its feathery bottle-brush plumes of rough greenery can create a jungle of growth which resembles a mini pine forest. On cultivated ground, where it is pulled frequently and burnt, it is more liable to form dense coarse mats. These must be removed with the utmost care because horsetail is prolific. It can replicate itself from the smallest fragment of filamentous top, and this can break all too easily. The tops are nothing compared to what lies below. Wiry black stems can extend massively out of sight. Dirty Nails is resigned to sharing his space with this amazing plant, but by removing it whenever it becomes visible he ensures that his horsetails are kept under control.

Nevertheless, both of these weeds have their good points. When allowed to ramble unchecked, bindweed produces beautiful pink, almond-scented trumpet blooms which are adored by bees and butterflies. Horsetail is crammed full of silica which, if brewed up in a tea, is reputed to provide a tonic for the gardener's tired joints and other inflammations when used to bathe the affected areas.

FROM DIRTY NAILS' JOURNAL
SINGLE TREE

On a hill
For all to see
An old and wise
Single tree.

In a field
On its own
A memorial of
Days long gone.

Time lost
And time to come,
The rising moon
The sinking sun.

Branches spread
To greet thee.
Happy and sad
The Single Tree.

Jobs to do this Week

In the Greenhouse

- Disinfect the whole place with biodegradable cleaner.

- Clean the glass well.

- Fix broken guttering.

- Disinfect shelving.

- Put potted-up globe artichokes in the greenhouse for the winter.

On the Plot

- Clear climbing French beans and runner beans to the compost heap.

- Dig out compost heap and apply the good stuff!

- Clear browning leaves and dead vegetation from the cabbage patch.

- Compost remaining cauliflowers which have gone past their best (are showing yellow curds).

- Check over kale.

- Plant out winter purslane in a warm and sheltered bed for early leaves next spring.

- Pinch out all figs on the tree which are larger than pea-sized, as they are most unlikely to survive the winter. Drape horticultural fleece over tree to protect from frost but ensure adequate air-flow.

- Cut and clear undergrowth in the orchard in preparation for bulb planting.

In the Garden

Planting Spring Bulbs

This week Dirty Nails has been busy planting spring bulbs in the orchard. He is very keen to naturalise numerous different species of early-flowering plants in his fruit growing area. The hope is that they will complement a patch of land managed for productive trees beautifully at a time of year when colour and associated interest are at a premium. He has added a mix of winter aconite, crocus (Ruby Giant, Blue Pearl, Yellow), and snake's head fritillary to the clumps of snowdrops which he planted 'in the green' during springtime. This combination of flowers should provide an eye-catching display from February to May. Bulbs and corms from cultivated stock are available now from markets and garden centres.

Choosing his selection of beauties is the easy bit and great fun. The hard work really starts upon getting out into the garden. Dirty Nails maintains a thick compost mulch for 3 feet (90 cm) or so around his apples, plums and pears to suppress weed competition. His trees are still young and as yet unproductive. However, he allows the remaining area of the orchard to develop unmanaged through the spring, summer and autumn. The succession of vegetation provides a dense jungle of interesting plants and flowers. The fascinating plot becomes alive with frogs, spiders, grasshoppers and next-door's honey bees to name but a few of the residents and visitors.

The preferred plan is to leave the site untouched until after New Year apart from formative pruning of the trees, and then tidy it up in readiness for the growing season ahead. This prevents nettles and willowherb from taking over. But spring bulbs prefer to be planted before winter sets in, so the task of clearing has been completed early in order to accommodate them. The debris can be stuffed into a heap by the side for a few months and used by small animals as a sheltered spot to hibernate in.

Dirty Nails achieves a natural feel to his planting arrangement by tossing handfuls of bulbs onto the bare soil and popping each one in where it lands. When the earth is soft, individuals can be pushed down to the appropriate depth with fingers. If preferred, a stick can be used to create a suitable hole to nestle the bulb into and then cover over. Crocuses and fritillaries are happy at about 4 inches (10 cm) deep, with aconites at half that. Aconites are best planted separately, on account of their tubers resembling small lumps of soil and being easily overlooked.

Watching the orchard evolve each year is a constant wonder to Dirty Nails. His aim is to create a place which provides food for the family and an undisturbed reserve for creatures. Scattering wild bird food on the ground throughout the coldest months is another way to cultivate interest. He finds that many seeds inevitably get passed over by his hungry feathered friends and grow up into an exciting mix of grasses and cereals which add yet more diversity to the eclectic collection of plants and flowers.

FROM DIRTY NAILS' JOURNAL
SWEET CHESTNUTS

A lovely bright cold day with a chilling breeze that puts a dewdrop on your nose, at the tail-end of the sweet chestnut season. Last year it was beech mast, apples the year before that. This year the heavy-bearer has been sweet chestnuts. Fine shiny brown fat things they've been, exposing glimpses of their bounty in the leaf litter at the top of Stoney Path. For over two weeks now I've been collecting these nuts each morning. At first a pocket, then two without even searching. Now half of one after a scratch around with my boots and a prod with my stick.

They've almost finished but at their peak I was joined by kids and mums a-scuffing along the path en route to school, enjoying finding 'conkers' everywhere. The kids would have all stayed longer but the bell beckoned and they were dragged on, running down the hill to catch up. Some didn't even know the nuts were edible. Just the thrill of their colour, shape and texture was irresistible, and the ease of their detection meant that everyone could gather their fill. It's not every year in these parts that home-grown sweet chestnuts can genuinely fill one's belly on any night in season, but this has been an exceptional year.

Jobs to do this Week

In the Greenhouse

- Wash and disinfect more shelving.

- Spray whitefly on potted-up globe artichokes with nettle tincture.

- Ventilate daytime.

On the Plot

- Carefully pick and store ripe Wagener apples (old American variety; should keep crisp and juicy, ripen December/January, keep until March).

- Continue weeding and clearing whenever possible.

- Check over the plot in lovely October.

- Plant spring bulbs in the undisturbed soil of a fruit garden or orchard.

- Plant garlic, Germidour and Thermidrome.

- Keep paths clear.

- Hand weed amongst the root veg.

- Plant daffodils under a hedge of filberts and cobnuts.

In the Garden

October 3rd Week

Strawberries

Now is an ideal time to lift and pot up strawberries sown in early spring for over-wintering in a greenhouse or cold frame. It is a job which has been keeping Dirty Nails busy this week on account of the enormous number of runners (new plants), sixty-three, that have been produced from the dozen plants which he grew from seeds. He cultivates Temptation F1, a variety which provides rich and tasty fruits reliably in the second and third years after sowing. The first season's produce is like a sneak preview of the delights to come.

Dirty Nails simply separates the young plants complete with their extensive root growth and lovingly snuggles them down into pots of a compost such as John Innes Number 2. These strawberries will happily while away the winter months with a little protection and occasional watering. Dead and browning leaves can be snipped off with scissors, but soon fresh greenery will start to show. If really severe cold occurs, precautions can be taken by covering the pots with horticultural fleece or newspaper. The plan for next summer is to create fruiting strawberry towers with metal barrels so Dirty Nails will be keeping an eye out for these on his travels over the coming months.

Alpine Strawberries

Alpine strawberries are altogether tougher customers. Plants raised from seed this year have cropped heavily throughout the hot months and have been a hit with visiting children. Dirty Nails always directs them to a patch of these strawbs which he nurtures in a shady spot behind his shed. Alpine strawberries are unaffected by the shortage of daylight. He is happy to give his young friends and relatives permission to pick as many of the keenly-flavoured little red berries as they can find.

To ensure another bumper crop next time around, and to steer hungry eyes and hands away from his more highly-bred, highly-prized variety, Dirty Nails will be using shears to chop all his plants down to almost ground level in the next few days. Because these essentially wild strawbs are so thick of growth he is always extra vigilant for frogs when cutting back. A measured and careful job will result in no amphibious casualties.

FROM DIRTY NAILS' JOURNAL
CATCH UP IN THE RAIN

There has been some serious weather of late. The ground is waterlogged and still it rains at 3pm. Twelve hours ago the skies opened. The rain fell as though every tap and water outlet had been turned on. There must have been streams and waterfalls everywhere judging by the mess this morning. Pine Walk has been cut up with gulleys in the gravel, which in turn helter-skeltered down the badger paths into Stoney and on to Tanyard. How long the resurfacing on Pine Walk holds up is a debate regularly pondered on by the dog walkers, fresh air seekers and workers.

Piles of poplar leaves, brown and smelly, have collected behind the wheels of every car in St James with other assorted rubbish. Drain covers are blocked, and parsnips sit in the ground down the allotment, cankered and rotting. Barton Hill is too wet to drive across, soggy to walk on to the point of taking footprints. A situation made worse by the trashing it received when the fair set up camp for a week and the rain fell non-stop.

The new supermarket is all but opened now. Shelves are in and lights are on, hoarding fences down. The petrol station opened last week, and was busy when I drove by not long ago. A lot of trees were planted up there. A mix of ash, ornamental maple, red-flowered hawthorn, some beeches. I have not looked too closely, but did watch with curiosity as the yellow-jackets plonked pot-grown twenty-footers in their holes and slipped around, knee-deep in mud, stamping in wisps of cotoneaster. Time will tell; hopefully it will be more good than bad. Maybe it is the constant rain washing away my hopes as well as topsoil, but somehow I doubt it.

Jobs to do this Week

In the Greenhouse

- Check over and ventilate.

- Do the last of the washing and disinfecting.

On the Plot

- Harvest Borlotti beans. Then compost plants and dismantle canes.

- Cut down asparagus ferns and burn.

- Hand weed as needed.

- Continue the chore of pot washing.

- Empty and store away hose pipes in a safe and tidy manner.

- Potter and observe.

- Train red-leaved grape vine, Viti's Brant, to wires on the south-west facing side of a shed.

- Spread thick layer of compost onto asparagus bed.

- Weed amongst leeks.

- Compost dead and yellowing leaves from cabbage, kale and purple sprouting plants.

- Plant spring cabbage plants if you can get hold of a few healthy specimens.

- Weed winter onions.

- Prepare a rich plot for broad beans.

In the Garden October 4th Week

Hoeing

Unseasonably warm and sunny days at the end of October are the cue for Dirty Nails to get busy with the hoe and tickle over his veg plot. Where rough digging a few weeks ago has turned over and exposed the earth, a new generation of weed seeds are germinating to create a faint sheen of green against the brown soil. It is inevitable that autumn digging will prompt weed growth and from now until spring, ground and weather conditions seldom combine to make ideal hoeing conditions. However, where uncultivated land has not been sown with a green manure, Dirty Nails is alert to pounce on any occasion which offers morning breeze and sunshine enough to desiccate the likes of speedwell, fumitory, groundsel and others which fall victim to his hoe blade. Although many weeds will not be annihilated, but simply pushed over and transplanted in another place, their swift development will be checked.

Occasional hoeing throughout winter in the conditions outlined, coupled with a spot of hand weeding, will prevent a mat of growth from colonising disturbed soil. Rough sods and clods will also be gradually levelled. Piles of leaf mould, compost or spent grow-bag medium can also be spread around thus. Dirty Nails always uses wooden boards to access his ground when doing this job. They are thick enough to spread his weight without bowing, and wide enough to work from comfortably. Two such planks at 6 feet (180 cm) long each are ideal and ensure that the moist soil is never compacted. They can be positioned as needed alternately so that damaging boots never need to come into contact with the precious earth.

Kestrels on the Verge of Winter

Whilst taking a five-minute breather to collect thoughts and wipe sweat from his brow on the warmest late-October day he can remember, Dirty Nails was treated to the awesome spectacle of a kestrel as it scoured the rough pasture which drops away into a valley adjacent to his patch. It was looking keen, on the alert for voles and mice.

The bird at first alighted a communication pole in the field and was viewed surveying the thick sward all around. Then it took to the air, flying directly before swooping up to fix its position in the sky. With wings held outstretched and flickering, tail fanned and adjusting its angle slightly in response to subtle alterations of the wind, it caught the sunlight like a hawk-eyed jewel set against the purest crystal blue. This is the classic kestrel pose, with feathered hunter seemingly suspended and almost stock-still, which earns it the country name of 'wind-hover'.

Dirty Nails watched through binoculars as the bird of prey glided to a new hunting spot and held its station once more. The world which opens up through the lens of field glasses is truly remarkable – the yellow of a kestrel's legs, the rich chestnut and slate grey upon its wings and back, the flecks of brown scattered amongst its creamy breast and underwings, the hook of its beak. These features are rarely so visible to the naked eye. And all this whilst tending his veg!

The happy gardener sat watching, his elbows resting on bended knees. Grasshoppers 'sang' from amongst the sun-kissed clumps of tussocky grass and deep orange-flowered self-sown nasturtiums lolled over the side of the compost heap. Their blooms hummed to the buzz of busy bees, with no sign of a frost yet.

FROM DIRTY NAILS' JOURNAL
HALF AN HOUR BEFORE WORK

Friday morning, 8am. All quiet in the house except the kitchen tap which drips quicker than the ticking clock, reminding me that I must get on and fix it. Cat on the table under a lamp, keen, alert, tail twitching, waiting for her breakfast. A lump of fish thaws outside in the yard in a pot of now less than boiling water. Apples and a tangerine in the fruit bowl next to an empty mug and a small bottle of beer with nothing in it. Some papers, a couple of cards, one received and one to go. Pen, pencil, personal diary, mobile phone, indecently large bunch of keys, and a beautiful pair of secateurs that look like they need taking out into the garden in a pocket. Sleek, sharp, pure in the hand and true in the cut. Cat by the door now, mewing softly for her fish. It is nigh-on five and ten past eight, time to lash on and get out the house.

Jobs to do this Week

In the Greenhouse

- Start to rebuild shelving.

- Re-stock with pots as and when they get washed.

- Bring in citrus trees for over-winter protection.

- Keep ventilated.

On the Plot

- Sow broad bean, Aquadulce.

- Wash soiled pots.

- Hoe open ground in dry weather.

- Cut back plot edges.

- Earth up all carrots.

- Keep spreading well-decomposed leaf mould and compost.

- Clean ground where runner and French beans were but leave the roots to rot down and release ample supplies of stored nitrogen for the next crop.

- Carry out hedge trimming.

- Tidy all vegetable debris which could harbour pests and spread disease.

- If the soil is wet, either keep off it or work from wooden boards to minimise damage to the structure.

October Veg on the Menu

Leaves and greens
Cabbage, January King
Cabbage, Pyramid F1
Calabrese
Celeriac tops
Leaf beet
Swiss chard

Roots, tubers & stems
Beetroot
Carrot
Celeriac
Parsnip
Spuds (store)
Swede

Salads
Land cress
Lettuces
Nasturtium

Onion tribe
Elephant garlic (store)
Garlic (store)
Leek
Onion (store)
Red onion (store)
Shallot (store)
Spring onion

Edible Flowers
Nasturtium

Beans, peas & pods
Chilli pepper (store)
Dwarf French beans
French beans, climbing
Runner beans

Vegetable Fruits
Marrow (store)
Squash (store)
Tomato

Fruits
Grapes
Strawberries

In the Garden

November 1st Week

Tending Figs

This week Dirty Nails has been putting his fig tree to bed for the winter. It is a job that needs doing before the first frost. His is a young specimen of the Brown Turkey variety, planted this year and being trained with bamboo canes as a fan against the south-west facing side of his shed. Figs fruit readily on the previous year's growth, even from a young age when their roots are restricted and in firm ground.

A number of small figlets have developed over the last few months. The sad truth is that any of these larger than a big pea have little chance of surviving into next summer and then swelling to form a delicious edible morsel. In the interests of encouraging other tiny embryo figs which are nestling in the angles formed where leaf joins stem, pea-sized (and larger) figs should be removed carefully with secateurs. Horticultural fleece can then be draped over the tree and secured to the bamboo frame with string.

Fleece is excellent for frost protection because while keeping the nip of cold out it still allows the tree to breathe. Dirty Nails wraps three layers of fleece over his Brown Turkey to keep it really snug until the end of next March.

Butterfly Boxes

Whilst taking his evening torch-light stroll around the garden this week, Dirty Nails found a sorry-looking butterfly sitting on the path by his shed. He carefully picked up the insect on the stalk-end of a leaf. It was a comma butterfly, which has ragged wing edges and a tiny white squiggle (the 'comma') on the underside of each wing. After a mild autumn the arrival of consistently chilly nights are the cue for these, and other over-wintering butterflies such as the peacock and red admiral, to seek out the warmth and cover of ivy-clad tree trunks and outbuildings in which to hibernate. The wildlife-friendly gardener can put up purpose-built places for them too.

Made of thick wood and resembling a birds' nesting box, butterfly boxes are totally enclosed apart from narrow slits to allow the insects access to enter and exit. A couple of holes (one either side) have sturdy plastic flaps which can be opened and closed. It was via one of these that the pretty little fellow was accommodated into safety and shelter. Dirty Nails has his butterfly box secured against a south-facing fence, tucked in amongst a tangle of honeysuckle. He relocates disorientated butterflies into it at this time of year so that they may hibernate communally (which they like to do) and in peace.

FROM DIRTY NAILS' JOURNAL
TIME CHECK

The clock struck for the top of the hour. First down the end of St James and then again, almost in time, from on top of the hill. Digging stopped. Back arched, ears listened and brain counted. To my genuine surprise it was only ten o'clock, a fact double checked on the mobile phone. For a moment it felt like I had gained an hour – a whole hour! – and, relaxing my shoulders, pondered on what to do.

A day is always a day; the passing of time only changes with alterations of light, weather and perceptions. To have an extra hour before noon feels like having two after mid-day. It is a precious commodity, priceless and worth using wisely. To appreciate the relentless movement of time is to know the value of life. To make the most of it is to live.

Jobs to do this Week

In the Greenhouse

- Continue pot washing inside if it is cold in the open air.

- Ventilate.

- Check charges.

On the Plot

- Plant globe artichokes into prepared ground at two-metre intervals.

- Dig up self-seeded butterfly bushes and pot up for friends or relocate elsewhere on the plot.

- Plant bare-rooted hazel trees anytime between now and late February.

- Transplant self-sown foxgloves.

- Cast a caring and thoughtful eye over the plot, noting Jobs to do this Week and planning in your mind's eye for next year. These ideas will change, but it is not a bad idea to start thinking into the future now.

- Apply potash from fires as a mulch around step-over apples and Morello cherry.

- Cut alpine strawberry plants down to their crowns.

- Hand weed amongst sprouting shoots of garlic.

- Cut privet hedges.

In the Garden November 2nd Week

Planting Elephant Garlic

Elephant garlic is a giant version of the familiar, strongly flavoured, powerfully aromatic bulbous herb. A well grown specimen, or 'head', of elephant garlic can reach the size of a man's fist. It usually comprises four to seven segments, or cloves. Each individual clove is often as big or bigger than a complete head of ordinary garlic. For culinary purposes it has a mild flavour, even when added liberally to a dish.

Tracking down a supplier for this interesting crop may take the home-producer off the beaten track but is well worth the effort. With top growth assuming the proportions of a leek (to which elephant garlic is closely related), it adds variety to the veg patch and more than a little novelty for garlic lovers at mealtime. Dirty Nails ensures a continuous supply by always growing more than he needs and using the surplus to divide and replant for next year. It is a job which he has been doing this week.

Elephant garlic thrives in rich, well-drained soil, so firstly he adds plenty of organic matter to the growing site which is already weeded and turned over. He forks the good stuff in. The bed is then raked level. Extra large stones are removed to a pile elsewhere because they could come in handy for any number of future jobs. Rows are marked out with string tied between canes 12 inches (30 cm) apart. Elephant garlic cloves can be placed along these rows at anything from 8 to 12 inch (20 to 30 cm) spacings. The biggest cloves need more space to grow to their full potential. Dirty Nails plants his at 10 inch (25 cm) intervals by plunging each individual into the earth up to the depth of his knuckles and then smoothing soil back over the top. All that they require from now until mid-summer, when the tops turn yellow and whither to indicate ripeness below, is to be kept moist and weed-free.

Dirty Nails is partial to eating elephant garlic thinly sliced and delicately grilled on toast for breakfast. Another option is to roast them whole in the skins until slightly soft, for a substantial addition to a winter feast.

Tending Ice Plant

Ice plant (*Sedum spectabile*) is a favourite with Dirty Nails on account of the way that insects, especially bees, flock to its sturdy platters of colourful flower-heads in late-summer and autumn to take sustenance from the nectar-rich blooms. This week, before frosts nip, he has been tidying up these plants in Mrs Nails' borders. He cuts back old growth and uses the lengths of stalk to take cuttings. Her fine specimens in the garden are showing tight knots of fleshy pale-green leaves right down at soil level. These are next season's display and will be quite happy left where they are. In really cold snaps, upturned clay flower pots placed over the tender bits will provide protection.

He takes the severed stems into the greenhouse. Some are even now displaying tiny buds from the junction of leaf and stem. Having sifted through the off-cuts, those selected for potting up are snipped into 4 or 5 inch (10 to 12½ cm) portions and pushed halfway into pots filled with a fifty-fifty loam-based compost and coarse sand mix. At this stage Dirty Nails is mindful not to put the stems in upside-down. Ice plant takes readily when treated thus, kept moist (but not wet) and given a hint of heat down at the roots. Each cutting should put out enough roots to be potted on in the spring.

FROM DIRTY NAILS' JOURNAL
DIGGING JERUSALEMS
IN THE AFTERNOON

Temperatures are balmy mild for the time of year. This working man is over-dressed in more than a t-shirt and top as he digs Jerusalem artichokes, self-seeders from last year's overlooked tubers that sprouted in the onion bed. There's a hefty crop too, which didn't affect the Stuttgarter Giants so no complaints. But despite the weather being a total joy now, mild calm after this morning's soft rain, it somehow does not feel quite right.

Maybe it's too easy to romanticise about Novembers past, to recall frosts that really came later and when getting damp meant being chilled through unless you kept moving. Perhaps I haven't ridden a motorbike for so long that the pain of cold feet and cold hands, the palaver of donning layer upon layer and still wishing for more at the point of darkness, has been forgotten. It could get that cold around five o'clock but for now, approaching mid-afternoon, it is perfect to stop and take stock in.

The dry 'bay' of Shaftesbury in front, The Wilderness sweeping into the hangings of Great Lane and long gardens below the High Street. Buildings perched on top and encroaching below at the next road level, Leyton Lane. Sullen grey definition that is the Town Hall, then Trinity and the wonderful green of St James, studded with young oak and beech in a twelve or thirteen-year old strip. A wild park for all people and all seasons.

Abbey School ducklings on a jaunt into town along Park Walk, luncheon-takers on the benches, hard to see and small as toys from my vantage point in the bottom corner of the allotment field by the badger sett in the brambles. Out in the country away below, hidden by a jungle of briars, the chunter and thud of activity in the Sewage Works. Ahead in the gardens of Frenchmill Lane, dogs howling and barking all of a sudden. Closer at hand, sparrows, robins, tits and finches, my favourite company as I toil peacefully. The Town Hall clock strikes two.

Jobs to do this Week

In the Greenhouse

- Ensure that compost in pots with globe artichokes and other plants is damp but not wet.

- Pot up ice plant cuttings.

- Not much else to do in here for now.

On the Plot

- Plant elephant garlic.

- Remove unpicked and shrivelled grape bunches from vines.

- Cut back and tie in vines.

- Hand weed amongst Jerusalem artichokes.

- Extract long wiry lengths of underground couch grass encroaching from the edges.

- Weed around Nine Star Perennial broccoli.

- Use woody cuttings to make sticks for marking rows of seeds sown in the spring.

In the Garden November 3rd Week

Pruning Apple Trees

This week Dirty Nails has been pruning his young apple trees. He planted them early in the year as 'maiden whips', which have a year's growth on M26 ('bush') rootstock. His tip-bearing Worcester Permain and Cox-like Sunset have made excellent growth over the season. Dirty Nails pinched off a small amount of blossom in the springtime in order to concentrate all the tree's energy into growing, watered them thoroughly throughout the summer, and maintained a thick weed free mulch of compost all around (but not on) the stem. Formative pruning now, just as the leaves have fallen, to induce the springtime sprouting of a clutch of stems (and in following years create a goblet effect of fruiting branches), involves simply snipping off the top third of the whip.

The Worcester has forked naturally so each shoot is reduced as for a whip. The cut is made with clean, sharp secateurs at an angle just above a strong bud. Care must be taken not to cut parallel with the back of the bud and also not to leave a length of stump proud above it. Any side shoots sprouting up the stem are cut back to one or two buds. This looks drastic and can feel like the wrong thing to do to such a young tree. If executed carefully and thoughtfully, however, it should produce a strong and balanced framework of both beautiful and productive branches in the long run.

Planting Asparagus

An asparagus bed is a worthwhile investment if this unusual veg is enjoyed in the household. It is considered a delicacy and with only a six-week or so season in May and June is very expensive to buy. A single row requires a width of up to 5 feet (150 cm) with 18 inches (45 cm) between plants. Asparagus is quite demanding of space if grown in any quantity. Nevertheless, a well-made and maintained bed has the potential to be productive for 15 to 20 years. At this time of year a site can be selected and preparations for planting (in March or April) can begin.

To this end, Dirty Nails selects a sunny, well-drained position and marks out the size of his bed with canes and string. It needs to be meticulously weeded at this stage. Once planted, digging out deep rooted weeds is no longer an option because such activity will damage the resident crop. Ground infested with horsetail, bindweed or couch grass is best avoided. Heavy soils should be made lighter with liberal additions of compost and grit.

Dirty Nails dumps as much leaf mould, compost, manure and wood ash as he can spare and then adds some more. Asparagus enjoys rich soil. Now is the time to get as much of the good stuff evenly spread out over the bed as possible. Seaweed can be applied too, if available, and will be much appreciated on account of asparagus being a seaside native. This is all rather hard work. With daylight hours at a premium Dirty Nails is content to leave digging it all in for another time.

FROM DIRTY NAILS' JOURNAL

HERE IS . . . !

Soft, dripping, residual dampness and mist greeted me this morning before the light, as I threw open the back door and felt the beautiful calmness that so often precedes daybreak.

'That supermarket' opened this morning. For months up Coppice Street there has been a whirling-dervish of activity. Like a giant vehicle from outer space landing virtually in the middle of town. It has arrived. Leaving destruction and chaos, shattered homes and displaced beings bobbing and struggling helplessly in its wake. But the lights went on, shelves stacked full to overflowing, workforce arrived early and grateful, everything got ready and set. So here we were and there they went. I could be seduced if I was not such a stubborn refuser. Taken along by the colourful, easy, fake-friendly ride. The 'thank yous' and the 'welcomes' making me feel valued and important; if I was actually spending money I would be.

There is change in the air, a difference that can be both seen and heard. The landscape, of course, bears virtually no resemblance to how it was. Even that is part of the pull this punter strives to resist. Yes, naturally I would love to explore, to revel in the soft lushness of a still-hot loaf of bread, baked especially and wrapped in something that seals that in-house goodness. To waft dreamily up and down the Technicolor isles, eyeing up all the goodies displayed wantonly for my perusal. To save and spend simultaneously. To live their dream.

But no, none of these things are going to happen. Just a bin-bag of sandwich cartons, broken glass, plastic drinks bottles and assorted chocolate wrappers. Some kind of tomato slice coated unattractively with some kind of dairy produce, the innards of a mass produced butty spilled out and trodden into the rubber matting under swings. How sad to see the new street lamps illuminated already, before 2 pm. How lucky I feel to have been the last person to mow this field when it was really a field, an overgrown sward of grasses, flowers, insects, birds and frogs. The old cricket field, or Guzzi field, survives only in postage-stamp form, one corner remaining. The rest, now half completely reconstructed football stadium and half petrol station and car park, lives on only in photographs and memories, sacrificed at the altar of progress.

Everyone is involved, interlinked, enmeshed, innocent or guilty to greater or lesser degrees depending on points of view and personal habits. That's life, and to simply live is to be a part of the whole trip.

Jobs to do this Week

In the Greenhouse

- Remove browning leaves from lettuces.

- Check over all plants.

- Clear gutters of collected fallen leaves.

- Avoid a build up of clutter by finding a place for everything and keeping everything in its place.

- Ventilate.

On the Plot

- Formatively prune apples and pears on M26 bush rootstock.

- Stroll out early with a cup of tea and listen for greater spotted woodpeckers drumming.

- Check over all areas on the plot.

- Tidy the shed!

- Snap off 'blown' Brussels sprouts so that only tight buttons remain on the stems.

- Fit protective plastic coils around the bottom of fruit tree trunks to protect from nibbling rabbits and voles.

- Drape horticultural fleece over globe artichoke crowns if frosty weather threatens.

- Uncover fleeced cabbages to do a thorough weeding job, then secure fleece back over.

- Prune step-over apples.

In the Garden

November 4th Week

In the Greenhouse

Dirty Nails keeps close tabs on the weather forecast at all times. Freezing conditions are his prime concern at this time of year. A cold (unheated) greenhouse may not be sufficient to prevent delicate foliage from being frost-bitten or pots from freezing solid in really severe weather. Fully insulating the greenhouse with bubble wrap is one option but can be a major job. It will also reduce the amount of light available to his plants. During the winter months this crucial element is in short supply anyway.

Nails protects his charges on those occasions when a chill really threatens by draping sections of horticultural fleece or blankets of bubble wrap over and around them individually (a 'floating mulch'). This is easily done and simple to remove, fold, and apply again as and when needed.

Dirty Nails always keeps a bucket or two of water in his greenhouse. This ensures that he has a supply available with the chill taken off for tending his under-cover plants. It is much kinder to their roots than very cold water.

Watching Lesser Redpolls

On one of those crisp, clear winter mornings this week, when a bright eleven o'clock sun had lifted the white veil of frost from all but the shadiest corners and hollows, Dirty Nails was entertained by busy flocks of birds as he cast a thoughtful eye over his plot. Grasping the head-high brown stalks of uncut stinging nettles, a small posse of lesser redpolls were having a feed.

These little finches are slightly smaller than a sparrow, with creamy-beige bodies and brown streaky flecks on their undersides. Sporting a distinctive red 'cap' on their foreheads, like a Moroccan's fez, they delicately extracted the tiny seeds from dangling tassels with frequent pauses to stop, look up and around and maybe wipe their beaks, before tucking in some more. The value of keeping parts of the veg patch unkempt and uncut cannot be over-estimated. When the weather turns hard many creatures are quick to exploit this natural larder. Dirty Nails is always pleased to see wildlife taking advantage of his 'stingers'. They are a vital part of the garden eco-system all year round.

FROM DIRTY NAILS' JOURNAL
BIRDWATCHING

How many towns can support flocks of long-tailed tits right in their centres? Shaftesbury still can, as I observed yesterday, in what is now known only as 'land off Bleke Street', but was a dedicated green space gifted to the town. Their mischievous twitters high up in a youthful ash alerted me and looking upwards there they were, flitting through the branches like specks of rain spotting on a window.

And now I sit in Cockram's car park by the Boys' Club, a small circle of tarmac with hawthorns, beech, pine, elm and elder all around. Being treated to the spectacle of chaffinches in a small flock, perching in the lower branches of a monster beech and alighting on the grassy verge to do what they do, then rising into the protective arms of other small trees. In and out they dart. One moves position. Suddenly they're all at it in a flurry, then calm again. There is great pleasure to be had in watching this amazing group of over a dozen hunting on the leaf littered ground for beech mast.

Until a lorry roars by on Christies Lane, and the sheer strength of its noise sends them up into the branches as one. The volume of man-made sounds right here right now is way over and above anything heard in this location before. The change is fast but on this morning, the tits and finches are hanging on still.

Jobs to do this Week

In the Greenhouse

- Purchase plastic bubble wrap of suitable size and proportions to insulate the greenhouse (measure first!).

- Keep slightly ventilated in mild conditions.

- Not much else to worry about!

On the Plot

- Keep extracting couch grass wherever it may be, and burn (do not compost).

- Harvest last of the beetroot.

- Spread leaf mould and compost onto bare soil on the plot.

- Pull off oldest lower leaves from celeriac to keep them clean and tidy.

- Earth up Late purple sprouting.

- Cover autumn-sown broad beans with fleece if cold weather demands it.

- Strip leaves from Swiss chard down to the fresh hearts and cover with cloches.

- Keep on top of the weeding now most growth has slowed to a virtual stop.

- Transplant rogue hawthorn seedlings into hedges elsewhere.

- Tidy yellowing leaves from kale.

In the Garden November 5th Week

Preparing the Asparagus Bed with a Friend

This week Dirty Nails has started to dig over his planned asparagus bed. Cultivating it to the depth of one spit (the length of a spade head) is sufficient unless the soil is very compacted, in which case 'double-digging' will be a back-breaking necessity. He ensures that the composts, manures, leaf mould and other natural fertilisers and conditioners previously spread evenly over the plot are well turned in. There is no need to break down the chunky clods at this stage as the weathering action of wind, frost and rain over the next few months should do much of the work for him. Come springtime the soil should be crumbly and fine, an easy pleasure to work with.

Whilst engaged in this work Dirty Nails has been enjoying the bold and colourful company of a cock pheasant. The bird has become a regular visitor of late, finding food and refuge during the recent cold snap. Pheasant, unlike asparagus, is definitely not on Dirty Nails' menu but nevertheless this large and very handsome fellow has a habit of running zigzag for the cover of some brambles when the gardener approaches. He waits in the wings awhile. Once content that all is well, he creeps out and cautiously stalks through a piece of rough ground, announcing his return with repeated short, rasping, barking honks.

On bare earth he struts and pokes about, with beautiful plumage that fairly glows even in the cold greyness of the late November air. His colours are divine. A white collar reveals Chinese ancestry (as opposed to Asian birds who lack this feature), with an amazing deep shiny green and purple head, bright scarlet eye patches and grey-brown crown. The pheasant's body is an iridescent mix of golds, browns, and glossy ginger-reds with a chequer-board of black half-moons upon breast and flanks. Perfectly proportioned with thick streamered tail, the bird nods and bows with each keen-eyed step, tossing and turning lumps of soil with his large curved beak.

When a five-minute shower of sleet passed overhead, the pheasant ducked under a line of standing runner bean poles and waited for the air to clear. He then picked his way boldly towards a double row of leeks. Having stood for a while, neck craned and alert for danger, the big bird bent over and concentrated on foraging for seeds and insects. By now he was oblivious to the close proximity of Dirty Nails who, fully water-proofed against the elements and bent double, continued to dig.

FROM DIRTY NAILS' JOURNAL
BARTON HILL BRIAR PATCH

There are not many days in these parts when the wind sweeps down from the north, but this was one of them. A cold fresh breeze that is a pleasure for working but not standing around in.

At Barton Hill there is a rough area which was, years ago, where a building stood that had something to do with the Football Club. In those days, the Rockies' home pitch was on Barton Hill Rec. Nowadays it is an overgrown tangle of brambles and nettles. Underneath the rambling vegetation is all sorts of litter, lobbed into the briar patch by countless unknown passers-by. Most folk who travel into town from the houses behind Ivy Cross walk past the vets and over Christies Lane, skirting the rough as they nip through a well-trodden hole in the hedge and across the Rec to Bell Street. A handsome elder tree stands in one corner unfortunately collecting beer cans and spirit bottles among its lower branches. But although many view the briar patch as an eye-sore, others see it as a wildlife refuge. A great place to tuck in to and hide away through winter if you are a frog. Deep in its heart, under the old telegraph poles, homes for un-noticed creatures that still find sanctuary up on the Rec. A thorny haven for birds, mammals and insects.

Today a fire occupied part of that spot. We burnt the accumulated brashings and cuttings resulting from work being done to crown lift the Christies Lane beeches. The fire was a roaring blaze but under control and neat. By the end of the day not half the woody waste was gone with plenty left to do tomorrow. Northerly winds kept smoke away from the incessant traffic. It billowed over towards the swimming pool and Barton Close instead. We ended our day happy and smiling, stinking of bonfires. At just about four o'clock an orangey sky across town promised more of the same but the word on the street is that tomorrow will be colder.

Jobs to do this Week

In the Greenhouse

- Keep the place neat and tidy, swept and cleared.

- After dark with the aid of a torch, remove lurking snails.

- Keep well ventilated.

On the Plot

- Potter and think as you have a gentle stroll round your little patch of heaven.

- Hand weed the leeks.

- Tidy old leaves and rubbish from the cabbage patch.

- Clear dead top growth from parsnips and swedes.

- Plant out pot-grown black knapweed, purple toadflax, Michaelmas daisy and foxglove where it will be of benefit to wildlife on the plot.

November Veg on the Menu

Leaves and greens
Cabbage, January King
Cabbage, Pyramid
Calabrese
Kale, Westland Winter
Swiss chard

Roots, tubers & stems
Beetroot
Carrot
Celeriac
Parsnip
Spuds, including Pink Fir Apple (store)
Salsify
Swede

Salads
Land cress
Lettuce
Nasturtium

Onion tribe
Elephant garlic (store)
Garlic (store)
Leek
Onion (store)
Red onion
Shallot (store)
Spring onion

Beans, peas & pods
Dwarf French beans

Vegetable Fruits
Butternut squash (store)
Marrow (store)
Spaghetti squash (store)

In the Garden

Tending Buddleia

The therapeutic value of gardening in this manic, rushing and tearing modern world should never be underestimated. For Dirty and Mrs Nails, an afternoon spent pottering about their little sanctuary amid another hectic end-of-year season is priceless relaxation. This calming influence can be heightened by tucking a sprig of fresh lavender into a breast pocket or under the brim of a hat, where the proven stress-relieving properties of this powerful herb can take effect on the wearer.

Cutting back Buddleia Davidii (the Butterfly Bush) is a job that can be done any time from now until early spring. This prolific deciduous bush bears masses of nectar-rich flower cones in mid to late summer on the current season's growth and responds well to a hard prune in winter. Untended, it is liable to get straggly and suffer from wind damage.

To this end, Dirty Nails uses a small pruning saw and sharp secateurs to lop off all the branches. Where he grows butterfly bushes as specimens around the outside of his plot, stems are removed down to within a foot (30 cm) of ground level. One plant is cultivated as the back-drop to a bench and over the years he has pruned the branches annually to form a thick-stemmed framework of splayed limbs. Having created the shape, all he does now is cut back annually to maintain this structure.

Buddleia Davidii will sprout from small dormant buds which abound at branch junctions and growth points lower down. Managing it thus stimulates a vibrant, lush and flower-full response come spring and summer.

Harvesting Kale

Dirty Nails is a big fan of kale (also known as 'borecole'). This brassica provides a winter-long supply of vitamin-rich greens for the dinner table. It is remarkably tough. Having tended his plants from seed sown in March, Dirty Nails is now harvesting on a regular basis. Varieties such as Pentland Brig and Westland Winter sport handsome crowns of large, thick, deeply crinkled leaves. They are easy to snap off close to the central stem. Cropping a few of the outer leaves regularly as required stimulates the production of more growth.

Dwarf Green Curled is a smaller variety and ideal for raising where space is tight. Sown a month after the others, it too is throwing out large frilly portions of tasty fare.

Kale is an easy vegetable to grow, following the seed packet instructions. Strongly flavoured, it is a rather poor relation to its more highly-bred and temperamental cousin the cabbage, tasting a tad more earthy and not quite so sweet. Dirty Nails always nurtures plenty of plants on account of their ease of cultivation, and the fact that they can be stripped bare of foliage by caterpillars in the summer but still live on and then crop reliably throughout even the harshest winter.

In the kitchen he checks leaves individually for snails sheltering in amongst the concertinaed fronds before sloshing them in cold water and steaming for a few minutes until tender. Even Young Master Nails, for whom most veggies are a no-go area, will ask for more when home-grown kale is on the menu, served hot with a knob of marg and twist of salt 'n' pepper.

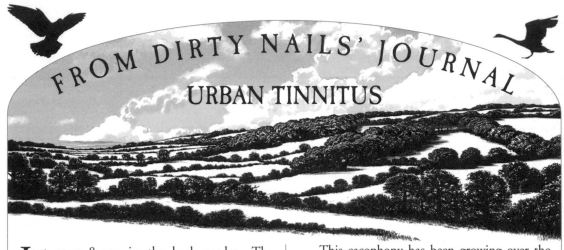

FROM DIRTY NAILS' JOURNAL
URBAN TINNITUS

Just gone 8 am in the back garden. The fascinating 'rat-tat' of a woodpecker working long-limbed branches of a big lime tree is muffled by the raucous urban tinnitus of rush-hour traffic up on top and away towards the Blandford Road. Fleeting glimpses of the bird are not enough to identify its greater or lesser secret, but the motorised aural backdrop is far more revealing: motorbikes, reversing service vehicles, speeding traffic, accelerating commuters.

This cacophony has been growing over the months, but since that supermarket opened something big has happened in the noise pollution department. Not in some anti-development imagination, but for real. As if some super-powered hand reached out from the clouds and turned up the volume dial on a radio of life about four or five notches. Peaceful early mornings may sadly never be the same again.

Jobs to do this Week

In the Greenhouse

- Tend lettuce seedlings.

- Ventilate in mild weather.

- Keep the place as organised as possible.

On the Plot

- Plant out wild flower seedlings, Black Knapweed and Ox-Eye daisy, in wildlife areas on the plot.

- Cut back butterfly bushes by at least half.

- Cut lanky vegetation and continue the job of weeding (which is far less hectic compared with six months ago!).

- Tend strawberry barrels by cutting back plants, cleaning and tidying.

- Stroll round the veg patch checking that all is as it should be.

In the Garden

Help from the Birds

A mischievous twittering overhead alerted Dirty Nails to the presence of long-tailed tits as he pottered and tidied in the garden earlier this week. Like a wispy plume of smoke caught in a gentle breeze, a loose flock of these gorgeous little birds flitted through a tangle of elder scrub and lime branches adjacent to his plot. These tiny tits are not only a pleasure to watch but also useful to have around. As they dangle like feathered pom-poms and perform acrobatics from twigs, they are actually picking all manner of insects and creepy-crawlies from inside crevices and under the bark. Dirty Nails is always delighted to be visited by these dainty black, pink and white customers, especially when the busy posse dallies amongst his fruit trees, cleaning them of pests such as winter moths.

... and Hinderance

This week Dirty Nails has been protecting his cabbage patch from hungry wood-pigeons. These brassica-munching birds often home in on such crops when cold weather strikes at this time of year. They like to sit quietly, all plumped up against the chill, patiently watching and waiting high up in surrounding trees. Frequently Dirty Nails disturbs their feeding as he strolls to the end of the garden. They rise in threes and fours with a noisy clapping of wings.

The tender green tips of purple sprouting and crowns of curly kale have been their favoured target of late. Although some losses are inevitable and not begrudged (pigeons need to eat too), the gardener must be concerned that continued damage (and also fouling of the leaves) will deny his exquisite pleasure of eating these greens at a later date. Conflict can be averted by erecting a barrier and Dirty Nails has been busy doing just that.

Plastic netting is perfect for this job. It can be purchased cheaply off the roll at most garden stores in 12 foot (3.6 metre) or 6 foot (1.8 metre) widths, cut to the desired length. There are many ways to drape this over valuable veg. Dirty Nails starts by pegging down two corners on one end. Then he carefully stretches it over the length of his cabbage patch and pegs the opposite two corners down also. He pushes bamboo canes into the ground by each peg and secures the netting to them with a twist of thin plastic-coated wire. Shredded carrier bags that rustle and flutter in the wind, tied atop the canes, are an added deterrent.

It is then simply a case of teasing the netting right over the whole crop and securing it low down with more canes and wire. Lightweight wire is ideal because it is easy to work with and strong. If tightly twisted below a bamboo knot it is sure not to ride up. Before it is secured all round, Dirty Nails crawls underneath with one more cane and upturned jam jar. This cane is positioned centrally, pushed down deep with the jar on top. The effect is to lift the netting off the greens, and hopefully stop the pigeons from simply landing as usual and pecking through the holes. Experience has taught Dirty Nails that these are highly intelligent birds and this battle for food is likely to be ongoing, especially if the winter is harsh.

FROM DIRTY NAILS' JOURNAL
SOWING EARLY PEAS

Yet more unseasonably warm weather yesterday got me all of a twitter and feeling the need to sow seeds. Peas are good for this time of year, depending on the chosen variety. I selected a packet of Feltham Early from the hardware shop, simultaneously boring and entertaining sales staff with excited verbal chatterings on the finer points of their cultivation.

The early morning alarm was set for 6 am. I was up and at 'em in the greenhouse with tea and torch by half-past. A roughly rigged-up lighting system was more than good enough. I was in solitary heaven as the rising sun illuminated the sky outside a salmon pink, working under a single light bulb, popping hard little dried peas into pots of home-produced leaf mould potting compost. An inch or so down, carefully pushed in with the flat end of a nail, fingers teasing the crumbly medium over and around, pressing down gently and lovingly.

Twenty-four seeds sown, twenty-four pots fitting twelve each into two trays. A tipple of water individually applied but not too much as the leaf mould, freshly dug from store down the allotment at the weekend and bagged up especially, was moist already. Trays set out on shelving units, labelled and looked at. If the family are eating home-grown peas in late spring or early summer, I will remind them that it all started here.

Jobs to do this Week

In the Greenhouse

- Clean the gutters.

- Keep well ventilated.

- Give a special 'winter feed' to citrus trees in pots.

- Check citrus trees for scale bugs under the leaves, and remove if found.

On the Plot

- Sprinkle wood ash on a prepared bed for shallots, and rake it into the surface.

- Clear and sweep paths.

- Have a warming bonfire by burning butterfly bush prunings.

- Protect greens from pigeons with plastic netting, especially Nine Star Perennial broccoli.

- Repair and revamp bird-scaring devices.

In the Garden

December 3rd Week

The Mid-Winter Lull

This week Dirty Nails has been enjoying the lull that mid-winter brings to his vegetable plot. Putting into practice his 'little and often' gardening philosophy ensures that a mild spell around Solstice can be spent doing barely more than harvesting crops as and when required, and daydreaming.

Growing veg successfully requires a consistency of effort and attention which can be both physically and mentally strenuous. After months of hard work, Dirty Nails takes enormous pleasure from this quiet time. As one year turns inexorably into the next, he re-kindles his energies. These short days have a magic all of their own. When the temperature lifts a bit, wind drops and sun's rays bathe the land in their gentle warmth, the garden looks utterly fantastic! With a patch of winter veg set against the glistening deep brown of recently turned moist earth, the sense of bounty and freedom can feel inspirational. Luxurious deep winter feasts of home-grown don't happen by accident; they have to be prepared well in advance.

With these and other thoughts in mind, it is a privilege to be outside 'in amongst it' right now. The neighbourhood song thrush is pouring out its beautiful tunes once more between late dawn and early dusk from high in its vantage half-way up a lime tree. Drumming echoes resounding from the woods nearby herald the onset of a new breeding season for greater spotted woodpeckers. In the orchard a mass of spring bulbs which were planted in the autumn are suddenly apparent, showing flashes of pale-green tips low down, scattered amongst the fruit trees. Dirty Nails checks on these daily, with the keen expectation of an excited child who awaits the arrival of a present-laden Father Christmas.

FROM DIRTY NAILS' JOURNAL
HERE COMES . . . !

3.15 pm, behind the police station. The high-pitched scream of chainsaws and the deeper tick-over of a heavy duty chipper. Grating thunder now and then as pieces of leylandii are pushed in by an earmuff-wearing worker and spat out in thousands of shreds. Behind the fence, boarded-up derelict houses and shattered ruins of sweet-smelling cypresses. Mechanical monsters. Men feeding them and working them. Nooks and crannies, refuges and creatures' homes, gobbled up in a crescendo of petrol-driven noise.

Grey sky above, cloudy with the odd hint of blue. Giant sycamores in a strip of woodland behind. Wild gardens being ransacked, people's homes readied for the ball and chain. Where will the blackbirds nest when the trees are gone? Where will the woodlice hide when the hidey-holes are smoothed away? 3.20pm now. There is work to do, lives to live in this chaos we continue to make.

Jobs to do this Week

In the Greenhouse

- Ventilate.

- Keep a fatherly (or motherly) eye on your charges.

On the Plot

- Check over.

- Clear remaining calabrese Marathon F1 to the compost heap.

- Move pigeon scarers to where they are needed most.

- Clear spent sunflowers and seed heads picked clean by the birds to the compost.

- Plant shallot Jermor sets.

- Hand weed around Jerusalem artichokes.

- Prop netting over kale to keep hungry pigeons at bay.

- Decant off marrow whisky by drilling through the blossom end of the fruit and straining liquid through muslin (in the shed). Enjoy it as best you can but don't have too much for the sake of your guts!

In the Garden December 4th Week

Rhubarb

Late December is a good time of year for tending clumps of rhubarb. By deep mid-winter there is no sign of life above ground, all lush stalks and leaves having long since been cleared away to the compost heap. Only a stick marks the spot. However, not far beneath the surface a large mass of thick, woody root is lying dormant with maybe four fat, squat buds (the 'crown') waiting to burst into growth come early spring. Rhubarb is a hungry plant and at this time of year Dirty Nails likes to give his charges some nourishment in the form of a thick mulch of well-rotted manure or compost.

Rhubarb can be considered a more-or-less permanent fixture in the veg patch. It will unfurl luxurious, expansive leaves atop thick, pink sticks year on year for many seasons. The sticks, with all leaf and woodiness removed, are useful in the kitchen from April until July for stewing, tart making, puddings and jams.

Although rhubarb will rub along happily enough left to its own devices it also responds handsomely to some tender loving care. Plenty of moisture in the growing season and a liquid feed of nettle-and-comfrey tincture from time to time pays dividends. Spare manure, applied as a top dressing, is appreciated at any time of year. Although this plant prefers to grow in a sunny spot it will tolerate an amount of shade.

The production of thin or sparse growth during the summer is an indication that the rhubarb is getting tired and is in need of a boost. This is done by digging up, dividing, and transplanting the clump. This exercise is most profitably carried out from December to February. Excavations that completely encircle and undermine the crown should do the job of removal. It can then be separated into portions, each sporting one or two healthy buds. Dirty Nails uses a saw at this stage as thrusting a spade into the root is liable to damage good buds. Any obviously weak or worn out pieces can be discarded to the fire site.

Bearing in mind the gross feeding and shading tendencies of this vegetable, each piece of root is best positioned 3 feet (90 cm) from its nearest neighbour. Planting holes should be enriched with plenty of organic matter. The more administered the better as this will provide nourishment for many a year. Heavy soils can be lightened with grit and wood-ash mixed in, while light soils are made more homely with extra composts and manures. Each hole should be large enough to accommodate the root, uncramped, with the topper-most bud covered by about 2 inches (5 cm) of soil.

No stems should be harvested during the coming season in order to allow the plant to become established and gather strength. Neither should rhubarb be allowed to flower in any year as the creamy bloom grows as tall as a child and weakens plants. Keeping a watchful eye on his crop throughout the summer, Dirty Nails will cut down to ground level any flower spike as soon as he notices the big bud issuing forth.

However, Mrs Nails Senior loves her rhubarb flower so lets it grow unfettered. She is minded to find a semi-shaded gap at the back of the border where she can enjoy the leaves and magnificent bloom as ornament rather than food.

FROM DIRTY NAILS' JOURNAL
MILD WEATHER
BEFORE CHRISTMAS

I disturbed a cabbage white caterpillar this afternoon whilst bending double and snapping off firm Brussels sprouts in the back garden. The yellow, black, white and green grub was low down, munching the bottom buttons. I left the critter where it was, although right through November and December others have been relocated from the white sprouting broccoli to the orchard.

Harvesting sprouts is always a momentous moment, a job that is looked forward to with expectation from the moment seeds are sown in spring. Sprouts are amazing plants, taking shape and popping out in all the right places like magic as the weeks pass. Strings criss-crossed over their tops, take-away cartons and shredded bark-chipping bags tied onto canes keep keen-eyed pigeons at bay. Now, in peak condition on the eve of the eve of the giant mid-winter festival, I have a bumper crop grown to perfection. A large bag of them was collected along with other veg for delivery down the road to sister-in-law in advance of the feast.

Later, as the church clock struck four, a mosquito buzzed my ear while I scraped my fork clean at the entrance to the shed after digging some carrots.

Jobs to do this Week

In the Greenhouse
- Ventilate when mild.

On the Plot
- Mooch and potter.

- Dig over any neglected areas planned for cultivation.

December Veg on the Menu

Leaves and greens
Brussels sprouts
Cabbage
Kale, Dwarf Green Curled
Kale, Westland Winter

Roots, tubers & stems
Carrots
Celeriac
Jerusalem artichoke
Parsnip
Scorzonera
Salsify
Spuds (store)
Swede

Salads
Land cress
Lettuces

Onion tribe
Elephant garlic (store)
Garlic (store)
Leek
Red onion (store)
Shallot (store)
Spring onion

Vegetable Fruits
Squash (store)

In the Garden

January 1st Week

Jerusalem Artichoke Fuseau

Jerusalem artichoke planting time has come around again. These interesting vegetables are members of the sunflower family and very easy to grow. Each plant provides ample supplies of distorted, creamy-coloured tubers for the winter kitchen throughout November to March. The problem with Jerusalems is that their twisted, gnarled shape makes them extremely fiddly and time-consuming to prepare, with a lot of wasted cut-offs. Dirty Nails has overcome this problem by cultivating a variety called Fuseau, which produces a clump of tasty swollen underground stems.

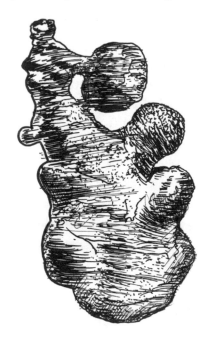

These are fat and oval in shape, if a bit bent on occasion, and are as quick and easy to prepare as potatoes. Jerusalem artichoke Fuseau is well worth tracking down from specialist suppliers.

Planting in early January will ensure a good return later in the year and is advisable as long as the ground is not frozen. Jerusalems perform well in sun or partial shade and in most types of soil that isn't waterlogged. They can scratch a living from even the most malnourished plot and will grow in places which are too poor for other foodstuffs. Even so, they respond famously to a little tender loving care. Because he enjoys eating them so much Dirty Nails is happy to lavish this on his 'chokes.

First of all, he lifts some of his standing crop and selects a few of the hen-egg sized tubers for re-planting. Ten will be more than enough for even the most ardent artichoke-eating family. Then he marks out his row with string tied between two canes. Jerusalems like plenty of space to fill out, so allowing 12 inch (30 cm) intervals between each plant and 3 feet (90 cm) between rows is not unreasonable. The tubers are laid out on top of the soil and then planted one at a time.

Dirty Nails does this by digging a hole as deep as the head of his spade. Three or four handfuls of spent potting compost or leaf mould are deposited into it, mixed in with a couple of fistfuls of soil. This is a hands-and-

173

knees job so he works from a wide plank to protect the soft earth and employs a kneeling pad to cushion his joints. It is a dirty job too, but great fun! Getting his hands deep down and plastered with cool muck so soon after New Year is a refreshing reminder of the earthy pleasure to be had from planting things. The tubers are then plunged in, one per hole, to a depth of 4 inches (10 cm). Care must be taken at this stage that they are planted with the shoot end uppermost. This is identified by the small pale cream bud at one end, which may have a pinky hue just below. The root end commonly sports a brown stub.

As they are planted Dirty Nails smoothes excavated soil over them and pats it down gently with the palm of his hand. When the task is complete he uses a rake to tickle over the surface, giving a nice neat and tidy finish. For the next few months all they require is to be kept moist and weed free.

A bucket of water and small scrubbing brush kept handy in the veg patch are useful for cleaning harvested Jerusalems before taking them indoors. A rich and flavoursome winter-warmer can be conjured up by slowly baking (use a lid) whole artichokes with red wine, olive oil, garlic, soy sauce and a splash of Tabasco

Wassailing

Wassailing is an ancient tradition which takes place on the day before Twelfth Night. It is intended to drive evil spirits away from orchards and fruit groves, thus stimulating a bountiful harvest in the season to come. Wassailing has its roots in the big apple-producing counties of Western England. Gifts were offered to the Goddess Pomona who looked after the orchard inhabitants. Cider was given to quench her, and toast to sustain her.

The ceremony itself has many local variations and customs, typically incorporating celebratory drinking, eating and dancing. In the olden days Wassailing was a serious and essential aspect of fruit husbandry. For Dirty Nails it is a simple affair which he conducts alone in the privacy of his own small fruit garden. It involves placing pieces of toast in the branches of his trees and dousing them in cider. He wishes each tree good fortune and takes a swig of fortified apple juice to accompany each blessing.

FROM DIRTY NAILS' JOURNAL
WORKING IN THE WIND
ON PINE WALK

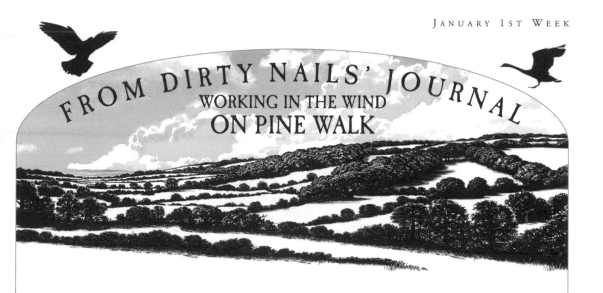

Under creaking, wildly-rocking, all-embracing, crazily-deformed branches of the Pine Walk beeches I sit. Down here on the ground a plastic bag tumbles and rolls along the gravel path like a dislodged tuft of seaweed travelling with currents on the sea floor. The calming influence of big trees is always apparent if a stroll is taken along this scenic route when the wind blows. Squeaks and groans from the towering sentinels as they tame a howling gale and filter it down to a brisk but pleasant dance of air around one's ears.

Today I'm here to water four Scots pine trees planted yesterday. They are handsome, conical young fellows, each no more than two feet high with a couple of whorls of branches and a strong green-needled leader. One even has a cone on it. With the principle of less meaning more, I have been working on Pine Walk a lot since the autumn - thinning out a dense ash and sycamore thicket, reducing coppice stump re-growth by half, removing dead wych elm, brashing untidy Scots up nearer St Johns Hill, knocking back bramble growth, keeping all hawthorns and hollies. What I like to think of as a subtle nip-and-tuck here and there. Enough to make the place feel loved but not so much as to offend or startle the eye.

And so, watering the pines is done. A vital job until they are established and coming along nicely. A pleasure to do, tending these young beauties and watching them grow.

Jobs to do this Week

In the Greenhouse

- Winter feed citrus trees.

- Wash dirty pots and trays in warm soapy water.

- Remove spent Salad Bowl lettuces to the compost heap.

On the Plot

- Sprinkle wood ash round base of fruit trees for a feed.

- Tidy around hazel hedges.

- Take measurements for any planned raised bed construction.

- Keep harvesting Jerusalem artichokes. Ensure every last piece is removed to completely clear the site.

- Check over all crops.

- Firm in shallots which have been uprooted by frost, birds, cats, or the lifting action of their own sprouting roots.

- Weed out willowherb and creeping buttercup.

- Plant thornless blackberry Loch Ness.

- Plant selected healthy Jerusalem artichoke Fuseau tubers in a freshly prepared site.

- Wassail all fruit trees with cider and toast on the evening of Twelfth Night.

In the Garden

January 2nd Week

Making Raised Beds

This week Dirty Nails has erected wooden boards around his veg patch. This has become a necessary measure on account of the amount of growing medium which was spilling out of his beds and onto the paths. It is a fact that continually boosting soil health by regularly depositing loads of leaf mould, compost and manure actually raises the level of the soil surface.

Tanalised (treated) timber both pleases the eye and is long lasting. Boards measuring 8 ½ inches (22 cm) by ½ inch (2 cm) are ideal, giving plenty of room for future bulking up of the good earth. For stakes, Dirty Nails cuts 3 feet (90 cm) lengths of 2 inch by 1½ inch (5 x 4 cm) tanalised square baton, sharpened at one end. A V-shape is much better than simply cutting the end diagonally. The stake will then go down straight, rather than curving in at an angle. A swan-necked hoe, tape measure, nails, screws, saw, hammer, lump hammer and drill are also essential tools for the job. Using a spirit level is optional. Dirty Nails prefers to trust his accuracy of eye. If things are slightly 'out' he does not worry too much.

First of all, measurements are taken for the size of bed to be enclosed and timber cut to appropriate lengths. He levels all the edges with the aid of a hoe. One at a time, he holds the cut-to-measure boards in place and taps them down slightly with a lump-hammer. A spare pair of hands is useful at this point but Dirty Nails manages happily enough on his own. Placing a stake on the inside, he knocks it in gently with the lump-hammer, using spare hand and booted foot to keep it upright and flush with the board. When happy with the angle and position, he bashes it down until just below the level of the board and secures them together by hammering in a nail.

Two or sometimes three stakes are desirable to secure these borders. Dirty Nails uses a screw to make each fitting solid and sturdy, working it in to a small 'pilot hole' drilled in advance. Where boards join, he places a short length of board on the inside which overlaps the point where they meet. This is secured into position with small screws carefully fixed in from either side. Corners are tricky but a stake which fits snugly at the right angle, with boards screwed to it, does what could be considered to be a good 'country job'. It is important to ensure that paths, when enclosed, are practical to work from. They must still be wide enough to push and turn a wheelbarrow, for example.

Small raised beds, which afford the gardener access to all areas by reaching over without needing to tread into, look great and make maintenance and crop rotation relatively easy. However, much ground-space is lost under paths. Dirty Nails prefers to enclose his big beds as one, and continue to work from temporary paths using lengths of thick, flat pieces of wood. These protect the delicate soil and can be moved as and when required. Neat and tidy edges and paths make a huge difference in the garden, be it flower border or vegetable plot. Dirty Nails is thrilled with his work which has both practical and aesthetic benefits. It has added definition to his growing areas and the paths are clean, uncluttered and inviting.

FROM DIRTY NAILS' JOURNAL
SYCAMORES ON PARK WALK

Blue sky above and beautiful trees. Away in the school playground a distant chorus of children's voices babbling. Dog barking somewhere underneath. Gentle hush of traffic rat-running along past the Two Brewers. I'm on top of Park Walk, morning sun on my back and leaning against the railings, looking up at three sycamores which stand beside each other nearest the top of Stoney Path. Their flaking trunks are festooned with tufts of lichen, thinning canopies, a mesh of crazy-angled branches and twigs that beautifully set off the sky behind. There's a noble essence that these trees possess, and the other trio between shelter and war memorial. Aged trunks rise up from tarmac skirts. They stand as remnants of a sycamore avenue that once graced this magical promenade. Now they await whatever fate becomes of them, on the down-curve of their circle of life.

Dignified, kindly hosts these trees. Housing for thousands of tiny creatures that are welcomed into the myriad nooks, crannies and hollows. Favourite haunts of the birds which eke a winter's ration from these squatting communities, sending a flotsam of pecked and scratched debris floating to the deck as they work tirelessly, which they must. Tits acrobatically at all angles hanging - blue, great and coal. Nuthatches like miniature woodpeckers, wearing their plumage of blue-grey cloaks and shirts of orange-pink. A pair of them, squabbling and tumbling through the branches, busy amongst dead wood within the crowns.

And then the flock moves on, prompted by a carrion crow that landed with a heavy rock and bob, sung a few throaty cackled notes, and wended his way too. The sycamores stand as if watching, waiting, like three old friends passing the time of day.

Jobs to do this Week

In the Greenhouse

- Ventilate in mild weather.

- Set out newly purchased seed potatoes for 'chitting'.

- Sow Early Pack 7 tomato, Pure Luck okra and Long Black aubergine if a little 'bottom heat' is available.

On the Plot

- Construct raised beds if this is what you want.

- Weed and tidy plot edges.

In the Garden

Dynamite Lettuce

The first clutch of snowdrops are showing tufts of grey-green leaves in the garden, their virginal white flower buds plumping up and drooping with simple, enchanting delicacy. With daylight enough after working hours bringing the promise of spring tangibly close, choruses of pinking blackbirds in the high hedges and banks around his plot, and a mesmerising orangey sunset on Tuesday, this week Dirty Nails has been sowing seeds and potting on.

Lettuces can be cultivated virtually all year round if careful selection of varieties is made plus protection from the elements provided throughout the coldest months. Dynamite is a 'butterhead' lettuce which can be sown in January and February under cover in trays. It is a hardy little fellow, resistant to aphid attack and generally free from diseases. A sowing made now and subsequently well tended should produce crisp, creamy, well-filled hearts early in the season.

Dirty Nails fills a tray with seed compost and levels it using a wooden firming board. He then makes small dents barely deeper than the thickness of a seed with the point of a large nail about 2 inches (5 cm) apart. Seeds look like quarter-sized grains of rice. Having emptied some of the contents of the packet into the palm of a hand, he deposits one seed per dent with the aid of tweezers, then uses the flat end of his nail to drag a little compost on top which lightly covers them. The firming board is employed once more, ensuring that the seeds are snuggled up comfy in their new bed.

All that is left to do, for now, is to keep them moist (but not wet) on a sunny greenhouse shelf (or cool windowsill in the house) and transplant to 12 inch (30 cm) spacings when large enough to handle.

Potting up Ice Plant Cuttings

In the autumn Dirty Nails popped short lengths of ice plant (*Sedum spectabile*) stems into pots of sandy compost. About half have survived. A warm hour was enjoyed in the greenhouse potting them on.

Nine small fresh pots sit on a shelf with wrinkled browny-black stems sporting grey-green clusters of fleshy leaves. New growth is paler green than old, and excitingly is sprouting here and there. Care needs to be taken in lifting prior to re-potting. Some bits of stem are sprouting delicate white shoots from below compost level. A small spatula, or purpose-made miniature trowel, is ideal for this job.

FROM DIRTY NAILS' JOURNAL
IN THE ORCHARD AT DAYBREAK

To rise about 6.30 and get out in the garden with a cup of tea as darkness gives way slowly to light is my pleasure at this time of year. To get outside the back door and hear song thrush greeting the early morning from his perched vantage in an elder bush on the Hangings lends a feeling that is not easy to describe. The first hour of daylight is arguably the best, as January turns increasingly into February.

A walk around the orchard, revisiting that special haven created from outbuildings and concrete, smashed and removed, then reconstructed with no restraining walls except a hedge and hazel hurdle fence. Free passage in and out for cats, badgers, birds and other creatures who share the space. A little spot for aconites and snowdrops to show themselves off before the self-seeded flower sward swamps bare earth. A secluded pocket of ground for apples, plums, pears and nuts to fruitfully grow. A magic corner of the Planet Earth Estate for me to work in, chill, watch wide-eyed and feel like a child again. A place to touch dreams in so many ways but not least of all by just sitting in quiet contemplation with an ear for the birds who entertain as the sun rises with a pinky hue.

To be with woodpeckers drumming on top and pigeons sitting in the massive lime growing within touching distance, to have many species of garden and woodland bird favourites, including bullfinches and long-tailed tits, is beyond any childhood expectation. Yet here they all are and I love it! An adored pocket of land. Totally, completely appreciated and nurtured with gentle care and respect for the life which it sustains. At times like these I can feel like the luckiest man alive, drinking in the emotions produced by life simply being lived and another day waking up.

Jobs to do this Week

In the Greenhouse

- Cover chitting spuds at night with newspaper or horticultural fleece to protect from frost.

- Sow small tray of Dynamite lettuce and Feltham First peas.

- Pot on ice plant and *Verbena*.

On the Plot

- Spread leaf mould and compost onto the plot and rake level.

- Do a bit of gentle hand weeding here and there.

- Tend celeriac by stripping off limp outside leaves.

- Keep digging Jerusalem artichokes.

- Do some hedge trimming if the mood takes you.

- Look out for frogs in the pond.

In the Garden

January 4th Week

First Early Peas

Fast-growing Feltham First is an ideal variety of pea to sow now in the greenhouse or on a window sill to secure an early summer picking during May and June.

The pale green dried peas rattle softly as Dirty Nails rolls them around in the palm of his hand. Discarding any showing signs of cracking or damage, he selects the biggest and cleanest for cultivation and nestles them snugly into 3½ inch (9 cm) pots of moist compost to a depth of 1½ inches (4 cm). A flat-headed nail is usefully employed firstly to make a neat hole appropriately deep, and then for gently easing the seed down and tickling compost on top for a neat finish. He places the pots in a sunny position and covers them with a pane of glass (or bubble wrap if conditions are especially cold). This will only be removed when the green shoots begin to shoulder their way out of the growing medium and reach up for the light.

This batch will be nurtured inside until late March/April, and then planted out in prepared ground or large pots, at 3 inch (7½ cm) intervals. Rich soil and minimum root disturbance at this stage are essential for subsequent production of large fat pods.

Dirty Nails doesn't grow vast amounts of peas. He prefers to bring on a dozen or so plants at a time to reap a modest harvest over a number of glorious weeks. This he achieves by making a sowing now and repeating the process three or four times at fortnightly intervals. The later sowings can be made direct into the soil outdoors.

A gardening highlight for Dirty Nails is to survey the burgeoning veg patch early on a warm May morning whilst popping a few pea pods straight from the vine, and delighting in the juicy sweetness of the green lovelies inside.

In the Garden

Planning for House Martins

May is also the month when house martins return to the neighbourhood. These fast-flying birds visit the UK each summer from tropical sub-Saharan Africa to breed. They are small, distinctively black and white in flight with a clearly forked tail which enables superb manoeuvrability, but they lack the long streamers sported by the related swallow.

House martins build amazing cup-shaped nests tucked under house eaves, constructed from stuck-together balls of soft mud. They may raise two broods of a summer but are less common now than in previous years. A combination of reduced insect numbers (due to increased pesticide use), rising levels of air pollution (to which they are particularly sensitive) and a lack of springtime mud for nest building (arising from changes in seasonal rainfall and general tidying up of dirty farmyards) has seen a marked reduction from the quarter to half a million UK breeding pairs of the early 1990s.

Late January is a good time to consider ways of helping this lovely bird to recover its numbers, and to this end Dirty Nails has fixed up purpose-built artificial house martin nest boxes under the eaves of his property. His experience is that a south-facing position is generally (but not exclusively) most successful. Although uptake may not be immediate, once they start to use them house martins will return year after year.

Nest boxes erected now will have time to 'weather in' slightly before the house martins come home. They are available, made to measure, from various wild bird food and accessory companies, and fairly easily screwed into position providing the eaves are at right-angles to the wall. As with all ladder jobs, a sensible risk assessment prior to commencing work and a reliable person to foot the ladder at all times is essential.

Dirty Nails is more than happy to invest the time and pennies if it means that, over the years ahead, he will have the chance to look up and be fascinated and entertained by the aerial acrobatics and dramas of one of his all-time favourite birds.

FROM DIRTY NAILS' JOURNAL
A JUNGLE OF DESTRUCTION

It's 10.30 am. I'm watching a giant orange digger grappling the big felled sycamore. The bucket is scouring bark from the trunks, tearing long cream wounds along their lengths. Shaking the tree and now swivelling it round, cracking, into another position. Like a hungry dog with a fleshy bone. A Rottweiler and yellow-jackets secure the site. All around lie broken ivied limbs and dismembered branches.

10.35 am, a chainsaw is cranked up, hidden behind the pile of vegetation. I suppose that now they are down, this strip of ancient woodland must be carved up into manageable portions for carting away, or the shredder. The digger is at it again, hauling out massive scarred tree bits and tearing it all apart.

10.39, and do you know what breaks my heart most of all? It's the little birds that flit between the fallen remains, looking for whatever it is that little birds look for in big trees. Catching the sunlight as they go, dodging in and around the jungle of destruction.

Jobs to do this Week

In the Greenhouse

- Frost protection for spuds.

- Ventilate daytime.

- Potter and tidy ready for the spring rush!

On the Plot

- Check over all areas.

- Tidy away junk and rubbish accumulations.

- Top dress Radar onions with wood ash.

- Clear and weed plot edges.

- Extract invasive couch grass and bindweed roots from amongst soft fruit bushes.

- Cover broad beans with fleece if the weather gets nasty.

- Maintain bird-scaring devices over crops, especially cabbages and greens.

- Tidy round Nine Star Perennial broccoli.

In the Garden January 5th Week

Seeds

This week Dirty Nails has been sorting out the coming season's seeds. Having survived for years keeping packets of his chosen varieties loose in a bag and shuffling through them as and when required, he decided it was time to get some organisation and common sense to his system. Now he has put them into alphabetical order and is keeping them in an open-topped box-tray. Pieces of card, marked and cut to fit width-ways whilst standing slightly proud, divide off the packets into alphabetical groups (AB, CD, EFG, HIJK and so on).

It is a wonderfully simple way of keeping seed packets in one place and accessible to hand. Dirty Nails is very happy to look at his planting plan (as he did this week), see that it is time to sow leeks in trays, go to his box, flit through the LMN section and easily find a small brown envelope of Carentan leek seeds amongst his lettuces, leaf beet and marrows.

Radishes

In the greenhouse, now is an ideal time to steal a march on spring and plant an early sowing of radishes. Dirty Nails does this by squeezing his into medium-sized pots with less than 2 inches (5 cm) between them. Radishes come in numerous different varieties to cater for all tastes and fancies but Dirty Nails is loyal to French Breakfast and is happy to overlook the rest (apart from China Rose which he sows in late summer for an autumn crop).

Having done his preparation, he empties a small quantity of creamy brown seeds into his hand and uses tweezers to select the biggest of that batch. He pops them in to a depth of no more than ½ inch (2 cm), moistens with water and covers with a pane of glass or bubble wrap. This will bring them on a tad quicker, especially if February turns out really cold. They will remain in their pots until the plump red roots are ready to eat.

Great Tits

Whilst inspecting standing crops and checking the progress of spring bulbs in the orchard Dirty Nails has also been enjoying the company of great tits. These active birds are frequent visitors, especially when food is deliberately put out for an assortment of feathered friends.

The largest of the seven UK species of tit, they are constantly on the move. Adults have a greeny-blue and yellow body with jet-black head and throat bib (which extends as a stripe down the chest) showing pure white cheek patches on either side of the face.

Great tits have a wide variety of calls but Dirty Nails listens out for their scolding squeak-and-chatter as they chase through the elder thickets, and a distinctive double-barrelled, bell-like chiming, 'tea-cher! tea-cher!' which brings even the dullest, greyest, cold morning to life.

FROM DIRTY NAILS' JOURNAL
SNOW DROPS

I think I can hear the preparatory work of building in town from first thing this morning. A distant hum of machinery polluting the tranquil St James air. Perhaps this is just the natural piped muzak of every day and I've only just noticed it playing as a backing track to the infrequent cars, school bus and the birds. They were led yesterday by the song thrush, and what a treat that was!

Anyway, today's the day, apparently, when the Coppice Street sycamores become history, so maybe senses are heightened to the ever-decreasing circles all around. It is peaceful enough here, on top of Jubilee Steps. The chocolate-box scene below, allotments, sewage works, rolling open countryside beyond stretching out seemingly forever.

My walk to work is even more of a treat these days, thanks to the snowdrops. Not twelve months ago we removed hundreds of these spring beauties from beneath those sycamores at the back of Coppice Street car park, for re-planting elsewhere. I took as many as I could, and dotted them around the Hangings and other small places. Jubilee Steps got a fair portion and they are coming out as I sit here now. A flush here and a blush there. For me, total heart-lifting eye-watering inspirational beauty every time; I hope a legacy that will increase year on year. One that will sit comfortably with the chirrup of the great tit, the cool of the breeze and the greyness of a late January morning.

Jobs to do this Week

In the Greenhouse

- In trays sow Verde tomatillo (with heat if available, alternatively on the kitchen window-sill), Premier cabbage, D'Orlanda corn salad, Carentan leek.

- In pots sow F1 Market Express turnip and French Breakfast radish.

- Protect chitting spuds and recent sowings at night if cold.

- Sow peppers if bottom heat is available: Ring o Fire, Saigon F1, Spirit F1 and Bendigo F1.

- Sow tomatoes Red Alert, Ailsa Craig and Tumbler for an early start.

On the Plot

- Check over.

- Potter and mooch.

- Remove globe artichokes in pots from the greenhouse and place in a sunny spot outside to harden off.

- Continue the ongoing task of clearing weeds.

January Veg on the Menu

Leaves and greens
Brussels sprouts
Cabbage, Savoy
Kale, Dwarf Green Curled
Kale, Thousandhead
Leaf beet
Swiss chard

Roots, tubers & stems
Carrots
Celeriac
Jerusalem artichoke
Parsnip
Salsify
Scorzonera
Spuds (store)
Swede

Salads
Lettuces

Onion tribe
Elephant garlic (store)
Garlic (store)
Leek
Onion (store)
Shallot (store)

Vegetable Fruits
Squash (store)

Veg on the Menu
Recipes

Veg and Onion Foogath

Ingredients
- Any pre-cooked vegetables, drained and chopped (cabbage, spinach, carrots, tomatoes, okra, beans, potatoes) – the quantity to be at least twice the volume of onion
- 1 large onion, chopped
- 1 normal-sized clove garlic, chopped
- 4 thin slices fresh ginger
- 3 green chillies cut lengthwise, seeds removed
- 1 tablespoon fresh coconut, finely grated
- Salt to taste

Method
1. Fry onion, garlic, ginger and chillies until golden (not dark) with salt if desired.
2. Add all the veg plus coconut. Continue to fry for a few minutes until blended.

Derek's Nettle Soup

Ingredients
- 1 bucket (about 250) stinging nettle tips
- 2 large red onions
- Several cloves garlic to taste
- 2 pints (1 litre) vegetable stock
- Drizzle of olive oil
- Seasoning

Method
1. Wearing kitchen gloves and using scissors, harvest the tender nettle tips before any flower buds are forming. Wash in cold water.
2. Drizzle a drop of olive oil into a saucepan, add the peeled and chopped onions and garlic, sweating until soft without browning.
3. Pour in the stock, bring to boiling point, and tip in the nettles.
4. Compress and stir with a wooden spoon before allowing to simmer for 5 minutes (it is this heat which takes the sting out of nettles).
5. Blend and serve, with black pepper, grated nutmeg, and the juice of half a lemon as optional extras.

Elizabeth's Elderflower Cordial

Ingredients

- Approximately 20 fresh elder flower heads
- 2lbs (900g) caster sugar
- 2oz (50g) citric acid
- 5 pieces of lemon and/or lime
- 4 pints (2 litres) boiling water

Method

1. Put caster sugar in a bowl of water and stir until dissolved.
2. Add citric acid and the elder flower heads, snipped off the stems.
3. Stir in thinly sliced lemons and/or limes.
4. Cover with cling film and leave in a cool place for five to six days. Stir daily.
5. Strain cordial through sterilised muslin (placed in a colander) into a bowl. Discard all solid matter.
6. Store in sterilised wine bottles. Dilute as desired with sparkling mineral water.

Spicy Noodles

This is really nice as a quick and filling tasty lunch.

Ingredients

- 2½ oz (65g) packet of flavoured instant noodles (curry, tomato or mushroom etc)
- 1 onion, chopped
- 1 tomato, chopped
- 1 green pepper, chopped
- Any other quick-cooking veg, chopped or shredded
- Little drop of oil
- Pinch of jeera (ground cumin)

Quantities and combination of veg is all to personal taste.

Method

1. Fry the chopped veg until nicely soft and cooked.
2. Add water (as directed on noodle package) and spice sachet.
3. Crush noodles into as small as possible pieces, add to water and boil.
4. Keep stirring. Add salt and pepper to taste when water has been absorbed.

Mooli & Carrot Salad

Ingredients
- Carrot, grated (quantities to suit)
- Mooli, grated (quantities to suit)
- Salt and pepper
- Squeeze of lemon juice
- Fresh coriander
- 2 green chillies (optional)

Method
1. Toss the mooli and carrot together in a mix, add seasoning, lemon juice and coriander leaves to taste.
2. As optional decoration use the two green chillies. For a strong flavour add chopped chilli complete with seeds. To encounter less of a 'hit', cut chillies lengthwise, remove and discard seeds, then chop and garnish with just the chilli pith.

Sliced Cucumber & Tomato Sandwiches

Ingredients
- Cucumber, very thinly sliced
- Tomato, thinly sliced
- Seasoning
- Margarine
- Hot toast

Method
1. Lavish pieces of toast with an even spread of margarine.
2. Lay the wafer-thin cucumber onto the toast slices.
3. Lay thinly cut tomatoes onto the cucumber. Take care not to overload; less is more!
4. Season to taste.
5. Top with another piece of hot toast and enjoy!

Aunties Sue's Summer Fruits Salad

Ingredients
- 8oz (225g) rhubarb, cut into chunks
- 8oz (225g) strawberries
- 8oz (225g) raspberries
- 8oz (225g) granulated sugar
- 4oz (110g) blackcurrants

Method
1. Cook rhubarb, blackcurrants, sugar and water together. Bring to the boil, stir well, simmer until tender (only takes a few minutes).
2. Add strawberries and raspberries. Boil for a further minute.
3. Serve hot, warm or cold (also freezes well).

Sandra's USA Tomatoes

Ingredients
- Big tomatoes, thickly sliced (however many you want!)
- Oil
- Salt and pepper
- Brown sugar
- White sugar
- Flour

Method
1. Dredge sliced tomatoes in flour, salt and pepper.
2. Fry in oil.
3. Whilst frying first side, sprinkle on some brown and white sugar.
4. When done, turn toms over, add brown and white sugar until done (becomes caramelised and has no tomato taste).

Mrs Tambay's Moong Dal Salad

Ingredients
- ½ cup moong dal
- 2 thick slices of cucumber
- 1 small red onion
- 2 radishes
- 1 tomato
- 1 green chilli
- Juice of half a lemon

Method
1. Soak overnight half a cup of shelled (yellow) moong dal, wash and drain well.
2. Finely dice cucumber, onion, radishes, tomato.
3. Cut green chilli thinly and lengthwise with seeds left in (chilli can be easily seen and removed prior to serving if desired).
4. Mix moong dal and all ingredients, add lemon juice and serve.

Strawberry Crumble

Ingredients
- 1lb 2oz (500g) strawberries
- 2½oz (60g) porridge oats
- 2½oz (60g) plain flour
- 1 teaspoon cinnamon
- 2oz (50g) margarine
- 2oz (50g) demerara sugar

Method
1. Cut any larger strawberries in half and lay evenly in the bottom of an oven-proof dish.
2. Mix oats, flour and cinnamon in a bowl.
3. Add the margarine in small chunks and rub in gently.
4. Stir in the sugar.
5. Sprinkle evenly over the strawberries.
6. Bake in a medium oven for 20 to 30 minutes.

Easy-Fried Brinjals

Ingredients
- 1 aubergine ('brinjal')
- Dhaniya powder
- Haldi
- Amchoor powder (dried mango)
- Salt
- Oil

Method
1. Slice the brinjal across into thin circles and spread over a plate or two.
2. Shake a dusting of salt over the slices. Leave to stand for a couple of hours so water in the brinjal has time to be drawn out.
3. Drain off all the liquid and pat dry. Sprinkle dhaniya, haldi and amchoor powder all over (less amchoor than the other spices).
4. … and fry!

Rice salad

Ingredients

- 10 oz (275g) brown rice
- 6 tablespoons olive oil
- 1 tablespoon white wine vinegar
- 1 clove garlic, crushed
- Salt and pepper to taste
- 1 apple, chopped into small cubes
- 2 spring onions, chopped
- Half a cucumber, peeled and diced
- 1 cup of peas
- 1 cup of sweetcorn
- Handful of raisins
- Handful of either cashew nuts or peanuts

Method

1. Cook the rice.
2. Combine the oil, vinegar, garlic, salt and pepper. Stir well.
3. Pour this combination over the drained rice whilst the rice is still warm.
4. Allow to cool.
5. When the rice is cold add all the other ingredients, toss thoroughly, and consume at leisure.

Red Cabbage, Date, Almond & Sunflower Seed Salad

Ingredients
Quantities are all to personal taste.
- Red cabbage, sliced diced and rinsed
- Dates, stoned and chopped in to small pieces
- Almonds, cut into halves
- Sunflower seeds

Method
1. Roast the almonds and seeds in a hot dry pan for a few minutes until golden but not burnt (burning a little bit is all right).
2. Thoroughly mix all the ingredients in a big bowl and serve.

Young Master Nails likes to add a wee splash of balsamic vinegar to his.

Moroccan Carrot & Orange

Ingredients
- 3 large carrots
- 3 medium oranges
- Orange water to taste (optional)

Method
1. Grate the carrots into a bowl.
2. Remove the skin and pith from one orange, cut into segments and add to the carrots.
3. Squeeze juice from the other two oranges over the carrots and toss together.
4. If using orange water, stir it in after squeezing the juice.

Mrs Nails' Warming Lentil Soup

Ingredients

This makes a huge pot, so for less just halve the ingredients.

- 4 garlic cloves, crushed
- 3 or 4 medium spuds, cubed
- 2 large onions, sliced
- 5 or 6 small carrots, sliced
- Any end-of-season tomatoes
- Fresh chilli to taste, finely chopped
- Sprig of lovage, rosemary, sage, parsley
- 2 bay leaves
- 1lb 2oz (500g) red lentils
- Vegetable bouillon
- 2 tins chopped tomatoes
- Salt and pepper
- 2 teaspoons brown sugar
- Half a lemon

Method

1. Sauté garlic and onions in a large pot until soft.
2. Add carrots and spuds, sauté.
3. Rinse red lentils in a sieve and throw in with the sautéed veg.
4. Add 2 tins chopped tomatoes.
5. Tie herbs together in a bunch with cotton and add with bay leaves and lemon.
6. Pour on enough water to generously cover lentils.
7. Sprinkle in 2 or 3 spoonfuls of veg bouillon.
8. Simmer until lentils are soft.
9. Press spuds and carrots against side of pan with wooden spoon to gently break them into smaller pieces.
10. Simmer slowly for about an hour.

Elizabeth's Spaghetti Squash Soup

Ingredients

- 1 Spaghetti squash, cut into chunks
- 2 red or white onions, chopped
- 2 garlic cloves, chopped
- 2 or 3 carrots, chopped
- 2 or 3 celery sticks, chopped
- Olive oil
- 1 or 2 teaspoons ground cumin
- 1 teaspoon caraway seeds
- Black pepper, to taste
- 1½ pints (1 litre) vegetable stock
- Toasted flaked almonds
- Cream (soya)

Method

1. Cut large Spaghetti squash into chunks and fry in olive oil in a large saucepan until softened a bit.
2. Add onions, garlic, carrots, celery and soften in a little more oil.
3. Add cumin and caraway seeds; fry gently.
4. Add black pepper to taste.
5. Add stock (increase the quantity for a thinner soup). Cook until all the veg is soft.
6. Blend in a liquidiser and allow to cool.
7. Re-heat and serve with a dollop of cream and toasted flaked almonds as a garnish.

Mrs Nails' Stir-fried Celeriac & Swede

Ingredients

Mrs Nails suggests trying this simple technique with any combination of root veg.

- Celeriac and swede (any amount, any combination)
- Olive oil
- Salt
- Pepper
- Lemon juice

Method

1. Grate or finely shred celeriac and swede.
2. Heat a little bit of olive oil in a pan.
3. Stir-fry veg until it begins to brown, moving around constantly with a spatula.
4. Add salt, pepper and squeeze of lemon juice directly before serving.

Parsnip, Cider & Butter Bean Soup

Ingredients

- Half a dozen shallots or a large onion, chopped
- 3 medium-sized parsnips, sliced
- 2 apples, cored and quartered
- Veg stock
- Cider
- Black pepper
- Bay leaves
- Thyme leaves, stripped from the sprig
- (Soya) margarine
- Tin of butter beans

Method

1. Cut shallots (or onion) into pieces and sauté until soft.

2. Add sliced parsnips and sauté for 10 minutes.

3. Add 50:50 veg stock and cider until parsnips are well covered.

4. Add apples, bay, thyme.

5. When 'snips have softened add the butter beans.

6. Cook until everything is lovely and soft. Add black pepper to taste.

7. Blend with a whizzer to chosen smooth creaminess. Add more 50:50 stock/cider to thin out if desired.

Colin's Cashew Nut Curry

Ingredients
- 3 onions, chopped
- 4 cloves garlic, finely chopped
- Good tablespoon or two hot Madras paste
- 1 tin coconut milk
- Button mushrooms as required
- Seasonal veg steamed (hard veg such as squash, parsnip, carrots, swede or Brussels sprouts are best)
- 9oz (250g) unsalted cashew nuts, crushed well but with some whole nuts in the mix
- 1 tin lychees with juice (or) pineapple chunks with juice (optional)

Method
1. In a big heavy pan, cook the onions on a high heat until soft and nearly (but not) burnt. Toss and turn continually.
2. Add the garlic, cook for 1 minute.
3. Add Madras paste, cooking and stirring for a further 2 minutes or so.
4. Keeping the temperature at maximum heat, chuck in the crushed and whole cashews. Stir well for a further minute. It should be a thick mix now and quite heavy going.
5. Pour in the coconut milk, mushrooms and steamed vegetables. Stir it all together and simmer on the lowest heat for no more than 10 minutes.
6. Optional ingredients can be added right at the end of cooking.
6. Turn off the heat and serve at leisure.

Mrs Nails' Creamed Parsnip & Celeriac

Delicious with crispy roast potatoes.

Ingredients

Use however many of these veggies you have to hand.
- Parsnips, cleaned and cut into chunks
- Celeriac, cleaned and cut into chunks
- Juice of half a lemon
- Salt and pepper
- Milk (soya)
- Margarine (soya)

Method

1. Mix parsnips and celeriac with lemon juice.
2. Boil until soft.
3. Add a knob of margarine, splosh of milk, season to taste and whiz with a hand-blender (alternatively mash until smooth).

Potato & Parsnip Rosti

Ingredients
- 4 medium sized potatoes, grated
- 1 parsnip, grated
- Margarine (soya) or olive oil
- Salt and pepper

Method

1. In small handfuls squeeze the liquid from the potatoes until they are quite dry.
2. Mix the parsnip in with the potatoes.
3. Season to taste with salt and pepper.
4. Heat the marg or oil in a frying pan. Spread the potato and parsnip mix evenly in the pan and press flat.
5. Cook until golden underneath.
6. Put a plate over the mixture. Turn the pan upside down, then slide the rosti back into the pan and cook the other side until it is golden too.

Mrs Nails' Ministrone Soup

Ingredients

Quantities are all to taste (any amount, any combination).

- Onion
- Garlic
- Seasonal winter veg, such as:
- Kale
- Swede
- Parsnip
- Hamburg parsley
- Spuds
- Carrot
- Leek
- Celeriac
- Herbs: thyme, sage, rosemary, bay
- Tin of chopped tomatoes
- Vegetable stock
- Fresh chilli, chopped
- Black pepper
- Tomato puree
- Olive oil
- Spaghetti, handful of broken sticks
- Jar of pasta sauce (optional)

Method

1. Sauté onions and garlic until soft and translucent (do not burn).
2. Gently sauté veg of choice, diced, in with the onions and garlic for 10 to 15 minutes.
3. Add chilli. Mix it in and sweat together with all the veg except kale.
4. Incorporate tin of tomatoes, pasta sauce (optional) and herbs (bound together in a bunch with cotton or string). Cover with stock and simmer on a low heat until all is soft.
5. Add shredded kale (or other greens) and broken spaghetti sticks. Continue to simmer gently until the spaghetti is cooked, then serve.

Mrs Nails' Swede & Red Cabbage Stir Fry

Ingredients

Quantities are all to taste (any amount, any combination).

- Red cabbage, thinly sliced
- Swede, cut into matchsticks
- Salt and pepper
- Juice of half a lemon
- Maple syrup
- Oil

Method

1. Heat a little oil until sizzling.
2. Throw in cabbage and swede. Mix together and stir-fry vigorously for a few minutes until cooked but firm in texture.
3. Season to taste.
4. A minute before serving up add a swirl of maple syrup and lemon juice
5. Continue to stir-fry for a couple of minutes, then serve straight away.

Mrs Nails' Medicinal January Stew (To ward off Colds and Viruses)

Ingredients

Quantities are all to taste (any amount; cut veg as you choose)

- Shallots
- Onions
- Leeks
- Garlic (suggest a whole head)
- Celeriac including tops
- Swede
- Carrots
- Parsnip
- Kale
- Good thumb of ginger, finely chopped or sliced
- Thyme and bay (a good sprig of these tied together in a little bunch with cotton)

- Olive oil
- Flour
- Spoonful maple syrup
- 1 tin butter beans
- Vegetable bouillon or stock
- Soy sauce
- Mushroom ketchup
- Worcestershire sauce
- Cider

Method

1. Sauté onions and shallots until slightly caramelised (do not burn).

2. Add garlic and ginger. Sauté a bit longer.

3. Mix in all other veg except celeriac tops and kale. Cook for about 5 more minutes.

4. Sprinkle in a couple of dessert spoons of flour while stirring constantly for a couple more minutes.

5. Gradually add bouillon or stock until all the veg is sitting in a creamy sauce.

6. Pour in cider to taste. Ensure all ingredients are generously covered.

7. Add celeriac tops, bay leaves and thyme.

8. Add mushroom ketchup, soy and Worcestershire sauce to taste. Keep stirring.

9. Put a dessert spoonful of maple syrup into the mix. Stir, then simmer gently for a couple of hours.

10. Later, add butter beans and greens. Add a bit more of this and that dependant on the taste you want.

11. Serve on a bed of mashed potato when the kale is cooked. This dish is best eaten in a bowl rather than on a plate as it can be a bit 'soupy'.

Glossary of Terms

ABDOMEN: part of an insect's segmented body.

AMPHIBIAN: frogs, toads and newts, which live on land but breed in the water.

AMPLEXUS: term used to describe the position taken by mating frogs and toads, with the male on top and holding tight.

ARBOREAL: living in the trees.

BEAN TRENCH: trench dug out to a spit in depth on the proposed site of a runner or French bean crop and filled with kitchen refuse before being covered over with soil a couple of months or so in advance of planting out a bean crop on top.

BLIGHT: fungal disease, especially affecting potatoes and tomatoes. May also refer to blackfly infestations on beans.

BLOWN (BRUSSELS SPROUTS): loose buttons on a stem, typically resulting from not providing a firm root run.

BOLTED: term used to describe when a plant flowers prematurely, usually due to extremes of temperature or irregular water supply.

BORDEAUX MIXTURE: copper-based fungicide used to prevent blight on potatoes and tomatoes.

BORECOLE: old-fashioned name for kale.

BOTTOM HEAT: gentle warmth given to seeds and tender seedlings, usually in the greenhouse environment.

BRASHING: term used to describe cutting off of lower branches of trees to about head height.

BRASSICAS: family name for members of the cabbage tribe.

BULB: tightly packed fleshy leaves, modified as a stem, which allows the plant to store goodness. The actual stem is at the bulb bottom from which the roots grow (called a 'basal plate').

BUTTERHEAD: heart-forming lettuces. Also 'Butterhead' is a named variety of this popular salad vegetable.

CACHE (FOXES): food store of surplus supplies hidden for a later date.

CATERPILLAR: the worm- or maggot-like larva of butterflies and moths.

CATKIN: the flowers of hazel. Male look like dangling lambs tails, female much smaller, bud-like, with tiny crimson star-like flower at the end. Appear typically January to March.

CAW (ROOK): word to describe the sound made by this bird, sometimes called the bare-faced crow.

CHARDS (GLOBE ARTICHOKE): side growths that can be cut off and potted up for future plants.

CHITTING: setting out individual potato tubers before planting in a frost free and light place so shoots may develop.

CHRYSALIS: the pupa of a moth or butterfly in the process of changing from caterpillar to winged insect.

CLOCHE: a clear covering for early and late veg production which is portable.

CLOVE (GARLIC): one of many strongly flavoured segments which make up the head.

COLD FRAME: box-like structure usually made of bricks, but can be wood, with glass top ('lights'). Used to nurture early or late crops, or as a halfway house for tender veggies between the protected greenhouse and open air of the plot.

COMPANION PLANTING: the act of planting different species together in close proximity for the positive effects they have on each other.

COMPOST: an organic materiel made up principally of decomposed vegetable matter.

COPPICE: the act of cutting trees and shrubs to just above ground level, usually on a rotation of seven years.

CORDWOOD: timbers cut into similar lengths (commonly 4 feet, or 1.2 metres) and stacked in a pile (or 'cord').

COURSE: to chase at speed by sight.

CROWN (GLOBE ARTICHOKE): base of the plant at ground level or just below.

CROWN LIFT: of trees, to remove the lower branches in order to raise the canopy.

CUCURBIT: family name for cucumbers, squashes, courgettes and marrows.

CUE: abbreviation of cucumber, commonly used in conversation as a term of endearment when talking about this member of the cucurbit family.

CUTTINGS (FOR PROPAGATION): portion of a plant cut off to be grown into another specimen. There are numerous different types of cutting (leaf, stem, root, bud) which may be taken at different times of the year.

DIBBLE IN: when planting leeks into their final bed, using a dibber to make a hole of appropriate size and depth to facilitate planting of the young leeks.

DIRECT SOWING: sowing seeds straight into a prepared seed bed in the open soil.

DOUBLE DIGGING: describes a technique where soil is cultivated to a depth of two spade heads ('spits'). May also be known as 'trench digging' or 'bastard trenching'.

DOWNY MILDEW: fungal disorder commonly affecting crops such as onions.

EARTH UP: to draw soil up around the base of a plant. Integral to potato cultivation but also applicable to leeks, celery, carrots and others.

ECOSYSTEM: a defined area containing all the living organisms and non living material.

ESPALIER, SINGLE TIER (APPLE): another way to describe a 'step-over' apple, grown on dwarfing rootstock as a spread of two opposite branches trained horizontally about 12 inches (30 cm) above the ground.

ETHER: the atmosphere.

FAIRY RINGERS: a Dorset name for bluebells.

FAN TRAINED: persuading a woody plant to grow flat against a fence or wall with branches spread as a fan.

FIGLET: term to describe a small fig.

FIRMED IN: using boots or knuckles to make soil around transplanted crops slightly compacted (essential in the successful husbandry of cabbages and Brussels sprouts).

FIRST EARLY (POTATO): quick maturing variety of spud which is ready to dig in June.

FLOATING MULCH: a protective covering on top of plants to resist the damaging effects of weather or pests, but not secured so it can rise with the growing crop.

FOLIAGE: the leaves of a plant.

FORMATIVE PRUNING: careful pruning of a tree in its early years in order to produce a specific desired shape or form.

GARDENER'S SHUFFLE: small sideways steps taken forwards and backwards to firm a bed, principally before the planting of onions or brassicas.

GERMINATE: what happens to a seed when it initially begins developing into a plant.

GOSSAMER: silk spun by spiders to make their webs.

GREEN MANURE: a quick-growing cover crop grown to replenish nutrients and body in a soil, to protect it, or all of these.

GROSS FEEDING TENDANCIES: the tendency of some plants to make high nutritional demands of nutrients in the soil (cabbages, for example).

GROW BAG: plastic bag containing compost specially formulated for the direct cultivation of a range of vegetables.

HANGINGS: steep slope which may or may not be wooded.

HAULM (POTATO): the leaves above ground (also used to describe stems and leaves of tomatoes and beans).

HEAD (GARLIC): whole bulb of garlic consisting of individual cloves.

HEEL IN: to dig a rough hole or trench for short-term storage of trees, leeks or brassicas.

HIBERNATION: to pass winter in a dormant state, for survival purposes.

HIT OFF (WITH A STRIMMER): cut.

HORTICULTURAL FLEECE: thin sheet of man-made fibre which is used to cover crops as protection from the weather or pests.

INVERTIBRATE: an animal without a backbone.

JOHN INNES COMPOST: range of growing media available to the amateur with nutrients tailored for specific purposes. For example; seed sowing (JI Seed), pricking out (JI Number 2), long term potting up of established plants (JI Number 3).

LATRINE: toilet area used by badgers.

LEAF LITTER: term used to describe the collected autumn fall of leaves from trees.

LEAF MOULD: the term used to describe leaves when decomposed and useful as a soil conditioner.

LINDEN: alternative name for a lime tree.

LINEAR (WOODLAND): referring to a hedgerow and its value as a long thin woodland rather than a compact area of trees.

LIQUID FEED: Plant growth stimulant in liquid form, typically diluted in water.

LOAM-BASED COMPOST: growing media based on loam rather than peat, comprising a good mix of different sized particles.

MAIDEN WHIP: one year old fruit tree comprising a single stem only.

MAINCROP (POTATO): spuds ready for harvest in September or October from a late spring planting. Also describes varieties of veg which produce the bulk of the crop in the main growing season.

MARBLED WHITE: unmistakeable black

and white chequered butterfly on the wing June to August especially in hot and dry summers. Largely confined to flower rich areas of southern England and southeast Wales. Caterpillars eat fescues and tor-grass.

MEADOW BROWN: common butterfly found throughout Britain and Ireland in wide range of habitats including meadows, woodland, coastal areas and urban places. Mostly brown wings with orange and single black eye spot on each top and bottom. On the wing from late May to early September. Caterpillars eat grasses.

MOLLUSC: an invertebrate with unsegmented body, in the garden referring to slugs and snails.

MULCH: protective layer of material placed on top and/or around plants to suppress weeds and conserve water.

M26 (BUSH) ROOTSTOCK: a 'dwarfing' rootstock for cultivating apple trees in a small garden. Trees should attain heights of roughly 10 feet (3 metres) to allow easy picking of fruit.

NETTLE AND COMFREY TINCTURE: home-made plant growth stimulant. The concentrated cordial of stinging nettles and comfrey.

ONION HOE: special small hand tool designed for use close in amongst a crop, principally onions.

ORCHARD: area of land set aside for the cultivation of fruit trees.

OVER-WINTER: crops which become dormant during the winter months as a survival mechanism, then resume growth quickly in the spring.

PALMATE (LEAVES): shaped like an open hand.

PASTORAL: rural scene of fields and hedges.

PILOT HOLE: small hole drilled or made with a pointed instrument to facilitate the insertion of a bigger screw afterwards.

PINK FIR APPLES: variety of potato which is small and knobbly, stores well and is best boiled and eaten cold.

PINKING (BLACKBIRD): distinctive chinking call of a blackbird, especially approaching dusk as they settle down for the night.

PLUMAGE: feathers on a bird.

POLLARD: a tree which has its branches cut back at head height or above to encourage fresh growth (originally beyond the reach of grazing animals).

POLLEN: fine powdery substance produced by male flower parts of seed-bearing plants.

POT GROWN: plants which have been raised in containers or pots.

POT ON: to move young plants which have outgrown the size of their pots into larger containers.

POT UP: describes the act of taking plants either from indoors or outside and growing them on in their own individual pots.

PRUNE: to remove dead, diseased, damaged or unwanted twigs and branches from a tree.

PUDDLE IN: drench the immediate area of the roots and allow soil to settle naturally (principally in leek cultivation).

PUNNET: small basket of fruit.

RIDGE (CUCUMBER): name given to cucumbers cultivated outdoors on raised mounds of enriched soil.

RINGLET: butterfly with dark brown wings showing faint eye spots on upper sides and conspicuous eye spots in pairs underneath. White wing borders are conspicuous especially in fresh specimens which may appear velvety. Frequents damp wooded glades and shady hedgerows, also open scrubby downland of England and Wales except north-west. Flies June to August. Caterpillars eat grasses.

ROCKIES: local name for Shaftesbury Football Club.

ROOT BALL: in container-raised plants, describes the knot of roots and growing medium in the pot or container.

ROOT BOLE (TREE): the part of the tree at ground level between roots and stem, which may be wide and spreading in some specimens.

ROOTSTOCK: the part of a grafted plant (usually a fruit tree) which provides the roots.

ROOT VEG: veggies where the edible portion is the underground root, such as carrots, parsnips, scorzonera and salsify.

ROSE (WATERING CAN): the spout fitting which filters water into a fine spray.

RUDERALS: short-lived weeds sometimes called 'ephemerals'. Pioneering plants amongst the first to colonise open ground.

RUNNERS (STRAWBERRIES): slender stems that spread out from the mother plant over the soil surface and forms new plants.

SALAD (POTATO): varieties of spud cultivated as Maincrops, developed specifically for eating cold after cooking.

SAPLING: young tree.

SCENT MARK (FOX): how a fox communicates its territory to other foxes by use of special glands and urine.

SECOND EARLY (POTATO): early maturing varieties ready to dig in July, after the First Earlies but before the Maincrops.

SEED BED: ground specially prepared to a fine texture for the direct sowing of seeds.

SEEDLING: the name given to a plant in the early stages of growth.

SIDE SHOOTS (FRUIT TREES): twigs and small branches growing out from the main stem framework.

SNUFFLE HOLE: describes the conical holes and shallow scrapes made by badgers in lawns and gardens as they search for insect grubs to eat.

SOLSTICE: can refer to the shortest day of the year (December 21st) or the longest (June 21st).

SPADGER: alternative name for the sparrow.

SPIT: in gardening terms, this refers to the length of a spade head.

SPORE: microscopic reproductive 'seed' of a fungus.

SPOT WEED: weeding selectively, removing some (but not all) weeds from an area.

SPUD: another name for potatoes.

STANDING CROP: any crops which are ready to eat and are stored where they grew until harvest time.

STUTTGARTER GIANT: variety of onion widely available for domestic production.

SUCCESSION: the naturally occurring development of vegetation towards a 'climax community' of woodland.

SUCCESSION SOWING: sowing varieties of veg at intervals, say fortnightly or every three weeks, to ensure a long cropping period.

SUCKER GROWTH: where a plant sprouts fresh growth from low down or at the end of cut branches.

SWAN-NECKED HOE: also called a 'draw hoe', useful for earthing up around crops or chopping off larger weeds at the root.

SWARD: turf or grass, or a stretch of turf or grass.

TATTIE: alternative name for potato.

TERRESTRIAL: land living.

THINNING: the act of reducing the number and density of plants growing in close proximity to each other.

TILTH: of soil, the fine and crumbly surface created by careful cultivation.

TINE: the slender prong of a garden fork.

TOP DRESSING: applying a material to the soil surface to replenish body or nutrients.

TRANSPLANT: to move a plant from one location to another.

TRAVELLER'S JOY: wildly occurring variety of clematis.

TRUG: gardeners basket, usually carried on the elbow or forearm.

TRUSS: compact cluster of flowers or fruits.

UNCERTIFIED STOCK (POTATO): potatoes which have not been certified as being free of disease, often appearing on the plot as overlooked and undug tubers from the previous year which grow as weeds.

UNGULATE: mammals with hooves.

WEATHER IN: of wood and other construction materials, so that they blend in naturally with their surroundings.

WHIP: see 'Maiden Whip'.

WILDLIFE-FRIENDLY: expression promoted by Dirty Nails to describe the practice of gardening with care and consideration to the plants and animals which share the plot.

Index